Praise for Eric Paul Shaffer's Green Leaves

"*Green Leaves* is fine. Think I'll make a pot of tea with these poems."

— Red Pine, a.k.a. Bill Porter, translator of *Dancing With the Dead: The Essential Red Pine Translations, The Collected Songs of Cold Mountain, The Zen Works of Stone House & In Such Hard Times & author of Zen Baggage: A Pilgrimage to China*

"Eric Paul Shaffer writes generous poems from a full, good heart and bright spirit— full of all the gratitude and wonder he feels at finding himself a mammal on this great Earth. Sadness and pain are here too, but they shrink in the light of these fine poems, which offer that rare balance of substance and accessibility."

— J.D. Whitney, author of *Grandmother Says, All My Relations & Sweeping the Broom Shorter*

"The piercing clarity of these poems acts as a 'window to this world' bringing its ordinary wonders into sharp view. Whether on a road to a city dump or a mountain pass to a monastery, Shaffer shows us that the quest is the same, to 'Live now' because this life is what we have. In line after remarkable line, the act of seeing and writing are woven into a powerful ethic of care for the earth because, as these poems remind us, 'We won't know what's lost until we can name what we see.'"

— Derek N. Otsuji, author of *The Kitchen of Small Hours*

"I have admired the work of Eric Paul Shaffer for many years, but to see it gathered in *Green Leaves* is stunning. These are pieces of wonder and wonderful pieces, the products of an open sensitive mind, of someone in love with words and the world and the love affair between words and the world. *Green Leaves* is a monument to what can be accomplished when a person dedicates their life to poetry and to paying attention. As I read it, I realized that I was muttering to myself again and again, "beautiful, beautiful, beautiful …""

— Joseph Mills, Susan Burress Wall Distinguished Professor of the Humanities at the University of North Carolina School of the Arts, and author of *This Miraculous Turning; Angels, Thieves, and Winemakers; Exit, pursued by a bear; & Bleachers*

"Can a New & Selected volume with depth and detail, image and imagination, breadth and breath also be fun to read? YES! Eric Paul Shaffer is the environmentalist of tomorrow, scrutinizing everything under the microscope and through the telescope. Read his poems today and be prepared for the future."

— Sara Backer, author of *Such Luck, Bicycle Lotus, Scavenger Hunt* & *American Fuji*

"Eric Paul Shaffer's deeply felt generosity towards his fellow humans is on display in *Green Leaves: Selected & New Poems.* The collection, spanning from 1988 to the present, reveals the patterns of Shaffer's engagement: encounters with the greatness of the universe balanced by everyday acts rendered poignant in Shaffer's careful hand; a celebration of life while looking unflinchingly at mortality; and, like many of the greats of American poetry, an approach that relies on humor and joy over sentimentality."

— Shawna Yang Ryan, author of *Water Ghosts* & *Green Island*

"How fortunate we are to have a collection of Eric Paul Shaffer's work that spans the full arc of his writing career. In this collection, we find a poet whose precision with language serves a restless and, yes, sometimes reckless heart. Shaffer dares to let big questions drive his work and to offer bold answers. He is a poet who is comfortable making readers a little uncomfortable while consistently offering clear insight and dynamic, lyrical phrasing. I find myself welcomed into the worlds of the poems and encouraged to see how Shaffer's striving for truth is always an effort to see the real world, the living planet, for what it is and to help us live a little better while we are here."

— Matt Daly, author of *Between Here and Home*

"'In fields great and green as new grain,' Eric Paul Shaffer leads us on one fantastical journey after another. Whether we are on the lush slopes of O'ahu or wandering among the colored squares of a Monopoly board, Shaffer guides us to the heart of each rich experience. Yes, 'holy is a bamboo cage in the human head,' but it's also 'the grandiloquence of stars,' a famous poet's squirming wife, a kid shouting from 'a platform, a podium, a pulpit,' the fun of bowling over dinosaurs with a portable planet. If Shaffer is doing anything right in these poems, and he definitely is, then it's 'finding the right things to love and loving them' until they're gone. Shaffer does what his rattlesnake does: he coils to center himself, 'nothing but the earth visible in the circle [he] makes.' And what an earth. 'Life is kind. Move on. Carry what you can.'"

— José A. Alcántara, author of *The Bitten World*

"'[S]tanding on the corner of Busy and Pointless,' Eric Paul Shaffer sounds his honest *'vox humana'* in *Green Leaves: Selected & New Poems,* a voice that is trustworthy because it's simultaneously humble and 'brilliant/and naked in its illumination.' In these pages, the poet beholds the grandeur of the world, naming what he can see on both grand and particular scales: On the one hand, a quintuplet of planets emerging in the same night sky and 'a mountain / shaped by fire and wind and rain and the mortal machines / of men' and on the other hand, 'the dull bronze curve / of the temple bell,' magpies 'on the verge / of the garden,' and mockingbirds 'listening to Mozart.' Whether in Okinawa or Oʻahu, Foodland or a monastery, the poet admits he's 'only human' and 'no more than any one of us,' but don't be fooled: His imagination brims with Shakespeare and Horace, Goethe and Ginsberg, its cup more full of humor and insight than Wallace Stevens's jar sitting atop a nondescript hill. For these poems overflow with 'hungry ghosts, magic kettles, / and lost desires of the holy' as well as of a 'superpower' that is anything but lame, 'lead[ing] the lost through the night surrounding us.' It's all about light, you see, from the rainbow hidden within himself 'like questions, like wonder, like his heart,' which 'shine[s] from within, inexplicably / and inexorably radiant.' In this collection of old and new work, Shaffer's inventive poetry delights and provokes us, as only the best art can do, transporting us to an 'intersection / of the ten directions—a solstice, a vision, a falling star, / an uncommon bird,' as it eclipses an all-too familiar sun, 'filling the sky with the light beyond the light.'"

— Julie Moore, author of *Election Day, Slipping Out of Bloom, Particular Scandals* & *Full Worm Moon*

"If this selected edition of Eric Paul Shaffer's many published volumes leaps all over, it's because Reckless, as his friends call him, has led a Pacific Rim life leaping from Soseki to satori, Bali to Cold Peak, Lāhaina Noon to bombed-out Kahoʻolawe. He casts his poet's eye on baseball-capped vendors, man-eating sharks, rattlesnake totems, brats in the schoolyard, Okinawa's thousand-yen bill. Basking in these reflections that conjure up stories and imaginings, Shaffer glows like a lyric supermoon with all the light he can't contain.

— Art Goodtimes, Western Slope Poet Laureate, Founder & Director of Talking Gourds, author of *As If the World Really Mattered, Dancing on Edge: The McRedeye Poems,* & *Looking South to Lone Cone*

"Eric Paul Shaffer pauses, looks, and looks again at fleeting shapes that crowd wobbling earth, taking the measure of a life encroached by kiawe trees, roiling sea, furtive loves, trips to Foodland and Walmart, and death in overalls, dying in jars beneath weeping stars. His mellifluous words grasp hold of mysteries that ground experience, insightfully affirming the meanings that linger in the sensations they evoke."

— D. Nandi Odhiambo, author of *Smells Like Stars, The Reverend's Apprentice, Kipligat's Chance* & *diss/ed banded nation*

Green Leaves

Also by Eric Paul Shaffer

Poetry

kindling: Poems from Two Poets, with James Taylor III   (Longhand Press, 1988)

RattleSnake Rider (Longhand Press, 1990)

Portable Planet (Leaping Dog Press, 2000)

Living at the Monastery, Working in the Kitchen (Leaping Dog Press, 2001)

Lāhaina Noon: Nā Mele O Maui (Leaping Dog Press, 2005)

Road Sign Suite: Across America and Again (Obscure Publications, 2007)

Restoring ~~Lady~~ Liberty (Obscure Publications, 2009)

A Million-Dollar Bill (Grayson Books, 2016)

Even Further West (Unsolicited Press, 2018)

Fiction

You Are Here (Obscure Publications, 2004)

The Felony Stick (Leaping Dog Press, 2006)

Burn & Learn, or Memoirs of the Cenozoic Era (Leaping Dog Press, 2009)

Criticism

How I Read Gertrude Stein by Lew Welch, edited and with an introduction by
   Eric Paul Shaffer (Grey Fox Press, 1996)

Green Leaves

Selected & New Poems

Eric Paul Shaffer

COYOTE ARTS

Albuquerque | 2023

Cover and interior design by Jordan Jones.

ISBN   978-1-58775-042-7 (paper)
         978-1-58775-043-4 (e-book)
Library of Congress Control Number: 2023941371

Coyote Arts LLC
PO Box 6690
Albuquerque, New Mexico 87197-6690 USA

coyote-arts.com

2   4   6   8   9   7   5   3   1

Contents

A Million-Dollar Bill (2016)

RattleSnake Rider (1990)

Lāhaina Noon
(2005)

Lāhaina Noon is the term chosen in 1990
by the Bishop Museum Planetarium
to designate the moment twice in a tropical year when the sun passes
directly overhead in Hawai'i
on its journey between the Tropics of Cancer and Capricorn

Lāhaina Noon

Today, I'm a shadowless man.
The sun calls me into the street,
and I walk alone into the light
of noon. The moment has come.

I stand quietly on Front Street
balancing the sun on my head.
My shadow crawls in my ear
to hide in the small, dark world

of my skull. The sun illuminates
the shadow in my skin, and I shine
like a second moon, reflecting
all the light I cannot contain.

As a Shark Sees

The Frenchman says he forgives
the shark. He lost
                five pounds of flesh
from a tanned leg dangling beneath a surfboard.
                He probably believes himself, but
he's lying. He wants to commend wildness,
but secretly he wishes for fins,
                craves to see the world
as a shark sees — through blue
from below a spatter of sunlight gold
pitched like pennies from hopeless hands.
                He wants to thrust upward
to the restless sky, to seek with his teeth,
                to tear flesh from empty air.

The First Man to See a Rainbow

— never told anyone.
Afraid it was only his imagination,
he kept the colors to himself, watched
the huge, hued arch slowly come and go,
        alone like nothing else in the world.

He could see that he could see
            through the spectral curve,
not only over and under but through
the tinted rings, and that made him doubt
        the rainbow was real.

Then, when he wished to touch
            the blunt flush of that red rim,
the rainbow retreated, remaining distant
as he approached, as though
        the touch of the man were death.

And the rainbow was nothing
like the horizon. He knew he could never
            reach that, but he could stand
in a place he had seen from afar,
        a place with new horizons.

Nor was the rainbow like the sun or the moon,
though those two were untouchable, too.
            Both bring light, and one heat,
and change the world, but a rainbow
        drifts between earth and sky like a cloud.

Yet even clouds cast shadows, and stars keep
changeless patterns and turn circles
    around the earth, but the rainbow
was nothing but a brilliant, beautiful, empty glow
   in a world made fresh by rain.

So he said nothing to anyone, never gazed
   at the colors in the presence of another.
He hid the rainbow within himself,
   like questions, like wonder, like his heart,
beating alone on curved dark ribs in a cage of bone.

Lovers on Pūlehu Road, Between the Sugar Mill and the Maui County Dump

His beat-up green pickup faces Haleakalā, her thrashed
Celica toward K-Mart, on the shoulder of Pūlehu Road. The lovers
                    stand in roadside mud, arms encircling

each other, gazing over a field of sugar cane at two boiling columns
        of smoke rising from the mill. They stand too close to be casual,

                    toes dirtied where they hang over the slipper's edge.
The afternoon reveals they should not be here, should not be
                    together, that only half their hearts attempt

to conceal their meeting. I drive past, but they do not look over,
                    knowing everyone on the island knows everyone else.

Not wanting to see themselves seen, their heads remain turned away.
My windows are down, and the stink of the dump rattles
                    white plastic bags tangled in kiawe trees.

I'm glad they let me pass without a glance. I don't want to know
                    whose wife she is or who his children are

or recognize a Safeway cashier or a meter-reader for Maui Electric.
                    My mirror shows unmoved lovers embracing
beneath ragged, windy limbs as trash cartwheels across the road.

                    They know the road to the dump is far too public
        for a lover's lane, and they have not forgotten their families

and their friends drive this red-stained, two-lane blacktop

to throw away what they no longer want, what they have used

beyond use, and all the many things they have broken.

Officer, I Saw the Whole Thing

a rant for Lawrence Hill, Albert Saijo, and Lew Welch

Officer, I saw the whole thing. I was standing there minding my own
   business, when the sky cracked open like a blue Easter egg, and
   suddenly, I saw it all
was made of atoms and molecules and elements bouncing around like the
   tiniest, infinitesimal, electron-microscopic drunks in the universe.
   Yes!

Officer, I saw the whole thing. I saw how every one of the six billion
   plus of us is just another *one,* not a carbon or a clone or a happy
   homogenized double half
of Mom and Dad, not another daughter or son in a long, boring line
   descending — and I do mean *descending* — from Adam and Eve.

No, Officer, I saw the *whole* thing. I saw every one of us as a miracle, each
   yet another one lovers groaning or giggling in the dark somewhere
   thought
they wanted, but nobody anywhere could have wanted or guessed or
   anticipated. Everybody is somebody nobody ever expected.

Officer, I saw the whole thing. Humans are just one little part of a big, blue
   watery world we call Earth — yes, 76% water, and *we* call it *Earth!*
   — and we're the only ones
who snarl at every other living creature, "Hey, move over! You were here
   first, but we can *think!* We're rational, you dumb animal! You can't
   think! You don't even count!"

Officer, I saw the whole thing. All the stars are suns, and light is a dream of
      darkness that touches nothing and goes nowhere, no matter how
      fast it travels through
icy emptiness, and I saw all of us made mostly of emptiness, more space
      than time, no matter how many watches I wear.

Officer, I saw the whole thing. I was standing on the corner of Busy and
      Pointless, and I was waiting for the light to change, when, as I said
      before, the sky split
like ovum cracked by a single sperm banging his head on the wall, and
      suddenly, there was everything hanging out for anyone to see.

And, Officer, I *saw* the whole thing. There were no fat doves to mistake for
      angels, and no white light, and no heavenly *vox humana,* and no
      streets paved
with solid gold, and no pearly gates, and no tunnel full of loco-motives
      charging me with one blind and blinding eye. No, there was
      nothing there at all.

Officer, I saw the whole thing, and yes, nothing was there! The universe as
      we know it is not known at all. It's a candy shell of red or green or
      brown or darker brown
or yellow or even blue — What's that missing color? Where's the new hue?
      — with *nothing* inside but our broken, little hope that something
      might be in there.

Officer, I saw the whole thing. When a guy turned to me and said,
      "Everything happens for a reason," I nearly screamed. My ears rang
      like school bells,
like church bells, like cow bells, like bicycle bells, like alarm bells, like
      somebody somewhere was talking stink about me.

Officer, I saw the whole thing right then, and I said "No!" to that fool and to
the orange hand holding me back and the ceaseless flow of traffic
and the starry sun
and the moony moon and the weeping stars and the grand cast of emptiness
in all directions. "No," I said, "everything does *not* happen for a
reason!"

Officer, I *saw* the whole thing — I mean everything at once! — and I yelled,
"No, everything happens because it *can,* and it *does,* and you just
can't stand it, can you?
Hell, you certainly can't *under*stand it! Nobody can. Reasons are for rear-
view mirrors, and 'Objects in mirror are *SMALLER* than they
appear!' A reason? Screw that!"

Officer, I saw the whole thing, and I shouted, "Keep your eyes on the road,
you fool, and watch where the hell you're going!" The universe is
just an accident
waiting to happen. Wait! Waiting? No, it's happening right now —
as constant as the speed of light times arbitrary squared.

Officer, I saw the whole thing, and if light travels 186,282 miles a second,
I see at the same speed, and I see every last person is a spectacular
cloud of molecules
like a rainbow nebula, like BB's in a box, and it's a wonder every wonderful
one of us doesn't flash with lightning, boom with thunder, and
burst with rain.

Officer, I saw the whole thing, and you were there, and I was there, and she
was there, and he was there, and they were there, and everyone was
there, and we were
all there, and we were all actually a real "we," yet not one of us knew what
anyone keeping an eye on the whole thing could easily see.

Officer, I *saw* the *whole thing.* Life is a live-music beer blast we all crashed
      wearing only our birthday suits. Life is a twenty-billion-year pile-
      up in thick fog and darkness
on a bridge over troubled *nada* — and not a tow-truck in sight. Life is *only*
      what we imagine, and *why* is that *not* enough?

Officer, I saw the whole thing. For one moment, the thing was whole, and
      then, it was gone. The concrete was beneath my feet, my head was
      still at the bottom of the sky,
and the exhaust was hot in my face. Horns were blaring, the sun was
      shining, and the rest of my life hung before me in the shape of my
      own breath.

Officer, I saw the whole thing, and it's all over. Nothing to see here, folks;
      it's all over now. Go about your business, people. Move along, move
      along now.
Yes, move along *now* because all I can see now *is* now. I came, I saw, I
      communicated. Yes, everything's all over, and here I am again, and
      I'm here to say:

Officer, I saw the whole thing, and it was one sweet, intimate glance at the
      ultimate. Now, I'm back, and I'm glad I'm back, and I'm going
      straight to my house.
I'll throw the front door open wide, walk in, and say, "Hello, sweetheart. Yes,
      it's me. I'm home. Happy Valentine's Day. I love you. Let me tell
      you about my day."

Victoria's Astronomy Lesson

The night's dark upcountry. Hold my hand tight. There's
Polaris, low in the sky over opuntia and telephone lines.
The astronomers say that when we gaze into the night,

we are looking back in time. All the stars we see are
not where we see them, and we are the only ones
to see those lights shine where they shine in our sky.

I smile because you're newly nine, and I'm time passing.
This little grin covers the fear and cheer in one less day
every day. Mine is an age when every moment marks me.

Tonight, watching that fat toad bounce his chubby butt
across the driveway nearly made me weep. I'm all right.
There's comfort in constant stars and a cool breeze

from the mountain. All the nonsense about time whines
in my ear as we open the whole starstruck sky together
and touch the constellations one by one. Astronomers

tell us everything in the universe is falling away from us,
and when I hold your hand, I wonder how I will ever find
the strength to let it all go, if I don't hold tight right now.

Whales at Sunset

At sunset, we sit on sand and watch whales leap from the sea.
The dying sun sets their breath aflame. The plumes gleam
for a moment before becoming a wind that blows ashore,
        casting sand in our eyes. Kahoʻolawe marks the horizon.

Behind us, Haleakalā rises like a wave surging to shore.
On sand surely the only testament of time, we linger over legends
                as light wanes. Centuries ago, the sea seethed
with the play of whales. Now, the ocean blackens with night.

Never has a day felt more final, and darkness comes
faster than light fades. As the sun sinks, shadow swells.
                        Every wave scales the shore
with the same determined hiss of triumph, loses strength,

and wanders back as the sea recalls the tide. Venus burns,
                then dives after day. There is nothing
to distinguish this dusk from any other. Yet there is
an end in this evening for which I am not prepared.

The tourboats are returning, black against dark waves,
points of light pale, but piercing twilight, gathering shadows
                        as foil for their narrow glow.
Free of us, the whales seek peace in the night below night.

As they winter in these waters, we hunt them, gawking,
pointing and screaming with delight, from groaning boats
                belching exhaust and dumping excrement
into the sea whales fill with song. I do nothing but watch.

I'm only human. I no longer wonder at myself and my kind
        who kill and call killing a living. As surf sighs
under stars scattered on the island's edge, I am resigned.
We are everywhere now. May night come swiftly.

May the whales never hate us as much as we love ourselves.
        And by the shore of this restless black sea,
these blue stars, and the waning crescent yet to rise,
may we kill ourselves before we kill the last of them.

Yet who am I to abandon humanity, one truth about all of us
none of us can change? I am no more than any one of us,
        no more right, no more wise, no more blind,
and my petty resignation is my own, a fate awful and just.

For athwart the stem at the whaleboat's bow,
        I would have held the harpoon myself,
and in the killing thrill of my kind, thrust the barbed iron
point deep into black and barnacled hide,

then crouched beneath peaked oars and gunwales,
full of fear and glee, while the struck whale ran
and flying line sang through the bounding craft
        and plunged smoking into the sea.

I, too, would have cast the blood of kin on cold waves,
and seeking the heart, driven the long lance into lungs,
        dyeing the sea with the hot, red rush,
darkening even the turquoise waters of paradise,

and after, I would have carved scenes of sailing ships
        at sunset on their teeth and seasoned bones,
and written poetry in the warm golden light of oil
        rendered from their sacred, slaughtered flesh.

One for the Bear

Walking a circle through every night sky I ever saw,
the bear was there. Always, the sun rose, then sunk
in a sky of rose, and the bear was there.

The moon clawed monthly through her deep,
black bag of silver change, and the bear was there.
Comets swept the speckled sky, then wandered

into cosmic wilds, and the bear was there.
Meteors scored the summer heat, and the bear was there.
He watched them fall. Every night, the sky was new,

yet never changed: the bear was there, rough, shuffling paws
tracking the year's long ring. The bear was there,
silent guardian of night's tiny gem. If the sky was black,

the bear was there, guiding eyes to the dim spark
we seek to find our way. The bear was there,
pacing a constant circle round the only steadfast star.

Mozart and the Mockingbird

This morning, I turned down Mozart to listen
            to a mockingbird perched on a wire
outside my window. Poor Mozart. Dead,
        he was much the worse for comparison.
But as soon as I lowered the music,
                the mockingbird flew.
        He had been listening to Mozart.

Telephone Lines

When the telephone first came to our upcountry farm in Kula,
there was only one wire. The numbers were a digit different,

but it was the same line. When anybody's rang, ours rang
in the kitchen, and so rang the receivers in every other house.
No matter what somebody said, anybody could be listening,

and everybody knew it, so nobody ever said anything important
or personal on the phone. Phones were public like a restroom

or a library is public. If the words were private, they were taken
outside or penned. Nobody ever called anybody for no reason,

and conversations were short. Before the telephone, we lived
alone where we couldn't even see the neighbors' lights at night,
but the wires shrunk the world. No longer was there anywhere

you knew anybody you couldn't call anymore. So we called.
Whenever we picked up the phone, there were voices in the line.

Ka ʻOkina:
Ka Leokanipū ʻEwalu I Ka ʻŌlelo Hawaiʻi

The eighth consonant is not a sound, but a paddle thrust
      through tides, a hole ground through an anchor stone

knotted to braided line rising through waves and current to sky
      and sun. The ʻokina is a hole through which the world speaks.

Here, the curl in the open breaking waves of vowels becomes
      a consonant carved of silence. On shores of endless blue,

where sea and sky trade hues, and islands are born from fire,
      the tongue must honor the silence within words.

A Blue Curve

On clear days in Kula, over the grassy ridge,
past the kiawe tree and a cloud-rippled headland,
                    we see the horizon where sky meets sea,
where light touches the dark blue,
                    where sea and sky come together
        in a line that marks the edge of the world.

As a boy, I was told sea and sky never meet,
                    the horizon is an illusion of our vision
            and the land where we stand,
that there are miles of emptiness and clouds
                    between two intimate, familiar hues,
        yet now I see there is no separation.

The sky starts where the sea starts,
                    face to face, skin to skin. In the surf,
        the sky coils within the arch of the rising wave,
wind sculpting wave, sea weaving sky
                    in a constant curl, each around the other,
                    on the long, luxuriant rush to shore.

Many are mistaken about the horizon, too.
                    The blue line bends too slightly to reveal
        the round, yet when we seek the horizon,
the gentle arc through every land and sea
                    leads us home. From here, our horizon
        is a blue curve in a world that encircles us all.

Even Further West
(2018)

"The islands are even further west than I thought."
— overheard in Lāhaina

A Boat of Bones

I'm on the beach, building a boat of bones, the long ones
from legs and arms, stripped of meat, slick and shiny,

as white as the sand where I kneel. I lash the bones
with sun-bleached twine, yellow rope, and a black cord
braided from torn strands of seaweed abandoned by tides.

I wish I was alone, but the poet squats beneath a palm,
his precious pages on his knee, scribbling literature

and telling me how to build a boat of bones. I don't listen
as he mumbles through blistered lips words I'm thankful
not to hear. Yesterday, he said, "One builds a boat as he

builds a poem, stave by stave." That means nothing to me.
I'm building a boat of bones, but I'm not caulking gaps,
for there is no caulk but damp sand, and this boat is built

to sink, not to sail. I'm hungry, he's hungry, and he's sick,
and we're both sick of fish. His eyes are sunk in his skull,

and seared red flesh burns through tears in his sleeves.
I'm building a boat of bones as I scan the horizon, stranded
with a babbler in rags who scratches verse in dim lines

on moldy pages, writing poetry with seawater and a stick.
"That boat is not worthy of the sea," he says, and he means

the boat will never float. Surf nearly drowns his voice,
but not quite. I'm building a boat of bones, and the last

I lash to the stern will be the poet's bones. Then, I'll drag
the boat through dunes, set the keel on the sea, thrust the bow
forward on a foam of broken waves. The boat will become

its own anchor and sink like one. I'm building a boat
of bones for the long voyage into the depths between me

and where I wish I was. The last of the boat I see will be
the poet's bones, flickering white, blue, gone, as the boat
sounds the fathoms I alone escaped. I'm building a boat

of bones, and when that craft sinks, the poet will be gone.
I'll sit silent on the sand and watch the empty sea for sails.

Headlights: A Biology Lesson

The sun gone, the green in the fields darkens. My neighbors drive on
without headlights, as if dusk were clouds of cane smoke and their vision
was improved by speeding past the burning stalks. Mr. Brown, our teacher
of biology and Drivers Ed., once asked our class a question,

"What are headlights for?" Someone snorted and said, "So you can see
where you're going." Mr. Brown scowled. That wasn't what he wanted,
so he tried again, "What is the most important use of headlights?"
When he put it that way, no one spoke. Everyone recognized a trap.

He rocked on his toes, waited long, and then gave us the words he wanted:
"So other drivers can see *you.*"
But speeding through oncoming night, these drivers don't want to see me.
They want to see an open road, a wild land, a new world, a paradise paved

for their wheels alone. Night conquers the world, and they want to think
they know where they're going. The cars, glossy but without color,
are no longer visible. Nobody can see them, and they can't see each other.
They fly over darkling land, crossing double yellow lines on blind curves

so they need not break the homeward rush. At my approach, the sullen flick
their parking lights to say, "I don't *need* lights. I can *see.*"
Maybe day fades at such a petty pace they fool themselves that they *can* see.
The road is familiar. They know every curve and dip, every weedy ditch

and lei-covered cross along the way. Most nights, they don't remember
driving home as they arrive, so they truly believe they don't need the light.
But I am cursed to recall Mr. Brown's brutal biology lesson,
the one where the frog lolls in a beaker of cool water with a thermometer

and a Bunsen burner below. The temperature rises gently to a killing boil,
so the frog never senses danger and slowly, stupidly cooks in the cauldron.
Driving home tonight, I see that's how darkness works, too: so gradually,
the light is gone before we even know we need to see.

Arrival

When you arrive, on the sand among ironwood trees,
            the tides, and last light, you can almost see where you are,
and you see arrival is an idea about getting somewhere,

            yet the place you arrive was here long before you were,
but then it wasn't a place yet. And it's not that you are
            the center of the place, like a dumb jar lolling on a hilltop,

            but arriving draws a place together like a web, a set
                        of radiating lines centering on you standing in the place,
looking around and finding a place to stand where every knot

            in the net sparkles like night suns waking over the black surge
of the sea. When you get to the place, your eyes start to focus,
                        to find a point of view for the place to regard itself

through your eyes. The place urges words into the air like stars
                        rising over the volcano. The place speaks with your voice,
            and the place makes you say, "Here, this is the place."

Illumination

On those cold, clear winter mornings, I rise in the dark and sit
        beneath a lamp with a pen and paper in a circle of light
barely bright enough for the work. The window beside me is black

and blank, and soon I'm staring only through the window of the page
at whatever I'm drawing from ink and concentration. Hours pass,
        and always, when I least expect it, there's a sudden tide of light

as the sun crests the mountain. When the first rays flood the fields,
the thin, yellow curtain behind me brightens, and the room swells
        with light. Everything is suddenly golden and illuminated,

and for just that one moment, I make the glorious and forgivable
        mistake of thinking it has something to do with me.

Witnesses

These two women call themselves witnesses. Desire drives
                them to speak of a place they cannot describe
without words someone else placed in their mouths. A myna

      squawks somewhere near, but everything else is still.
Even the road is silent. The door between us is locked.
      I smile at them through the screen, but I will not allow

them to enter, though the scent of roses fills the air between us.
      The bush by the porch is blooming. Neither the sun
nor the drought nor whatever chews holes in new green leaves

      can kill that tough stalk of thorns. These women yearn
to speak of saviors on a day when the concrete is mute at noon
      and the air too parched to spin a mirage from the ridge.

      I know enough of kindness to leave them
to their tragic metaphysics. One I love is dying, and these two

      know nothing of grief when death is final, immutable,
irrevocable. Heat like this might teach them if they were more
      than only lonely, and even traveling together, alone.

Above their upturned faces, the wasps work at the nest, mold
          a living beneath the eaves from paper and spit,
and these women hover now near my door as if at any moment

they might embark on a flood-borne vessel. The temperature
      stands at 88. They carry pamphlets and scripture bound
in hope and cowhide. No matter what they say, I'll never know

more of hell than they will. Behind them, weeds are
the only green in a field scorched grim and gold. The sky is blue
flame, and the mountain bears the light like a burden.

All There Is

for Jon and Thierry

Winter in paradise this year is dry enough to call a drought.
      The grass isn't green and isn't growing in the season

      we call the rainy one. No clouds color sunrise,
and every night, stars deepen the sky. Ancient light rains
from cloudless darkness. If there were enough for everyone,

      the rays wouldn't travel so fast. Light is a constant
reminder of the yearning between stars and all the worlds

      spinning in darkness, like this one, the one we love.
For this brown grass and the open space between stars,
      there's not much rain. Never will there be too much

or even enough, so we celebrate and celebrate fiercely
      all there is. When the rain finally comes, I'll stand

in the storm with my face raised. When the night comes,
I'll lift my eyes to the light and take it in. Rain will grace us,
      and stars will burn. Light flies through the night,

and rain finds the earth for no reason we know, yet we leap
      to drink our fill of what falls from above to sustain us.

Redemption

Someone convinced me that to praise Jesus, I should visit someone
languishing in jail, so I slunk my way downtown to Oh-Triple-See.
For all anybody knows, those letters could mean Oklahoma City
Community College or even Orange County Conservation Corps,
but they don't. They mean O'ahu Community Correctional Center.

The barbed wire and concrete walls are on a boulevard in Honolulu,
catty-corner from a recycling and redemption place: a nickel, a can.
I guess redemption keeps the streets fairly clean. That's a good thing.
So there I was. The clanging and slamming of steel was as musical

as it was peaceful. At random, a cheerful guard picked me a prisoner,
one with no visitors since intake. Frisked and X-rayed to invisibility,
I stared through lipstick-smudged, bullet-proof glass at one mean guy.
What could I say? I picked up the phone. So did he, a weird mirror
of reflections, shifting, and bent elbows. Warned to avoid the personal,

my tongue was tied to details of his incarceration, and they weren't
pretty. Grand larceny, drugs, domestic abuse: this guy was no friend
to Jesus, and not to me either. He asked what the hell I was doing here.
I wanted to know, too, so I asked him what he thought. He thought

I was an asshole or a fag. All his sentences included the word "fuck"
three or four times as a noun, verb, adjective, adverb, or interjection,
and I'm not used to that sort of language. Few words actually function
fully as five parts of speech. He just didn't care. To kill some time,
I asked him what he wanted, and he asked me what the hell I thought

he wanted. I was justifiably piqued by then, so I guessed he wanted a li-hing-mui-sprinkled cherry slush from Byron's because I was sure that's what I wanted. He was surprised, but then ardently advised me to encounter myself sexually. By then, I'd had enough bad humor,

so I hung up and stood up. He banged his erect middle finger loudly on the glass, and I wondered if the print on that very tip was the one to clinch his conviction. How ironic. He ordered me to stay, I left, and he cursed me because I could. Jesus or not, I had done my time. In my trunk, I'd crammed three reeking garbage bags of empty cans.

Of Owls and Sugar Cane

Outraged, the local newspaper reports a tragic death of Pueo,
          owl native to the islands, slammed from the sky
with fender, windshield, or grille. Yet a quick study of the photo

reveals a Barn Owl, limp with wing unfurled on a roadside
          where tall green stalks of cane rise behind the tidy pile

of feathers among the scattered trash. Of course, the bird
was a Barn Owl. They dive from the dark into headlights
          to strike mice the sudden day illuminates,

and drivers, eyes vacant with fatigue and too much familiarity
          with humming red roads, tear pale wings from stars

and cast hollow bones into the ditch. These drivers don't care
          what they hit and never stop to see. We are like them.

We won't know what's lost until we can name what we see.
          And we'll never know what will grow if we don't know

when or how to plant what the moon demands. Till the wheels
stop, we and our children will see no more in the earth but sugar
          and graves and the nameless grasses that cover them.

Five Planets at Once

"Come on outside," he said. "Tonight,
             you can see five planets at once."

He was grinning, with the sort of secret a brother keeps.
        "There's no moon. They should be easy to see."

In the field, eye-deep in the night, he pointed into the dark.

"The big white one up there is Jupiter. Some people can see
                three or four moons without a telescope.
                        That butter-colored one is Saturn."

"There's Mars. It's a little faint, but if you look hard,
                            you can see the red color.
            The brilliant one right over the mountain is Venus."

Then, he was silent. We stared together at a sky glowing
                    with the other worlds ringing our sun.
            Wind and small animals rustled in the grass.

"Hey," I said, "I thought you said we could see five planets."
                        "We can."

"Well, look. Jupiter, Saturn, Mars, and Venus is only four."
                    "That's right."

I could hear the smile in his voice. I thought for a moment,
        but not long enough. "So what's the other one?"

            He chuckled, and said, "Earth."

Sitting in the Last of Sunset, Listening to Guests Within

All my friends are in the kitchen now. Dinner is done, the sun set,
and after our muted admiration from the yard, by ones and twos,
they rose beneath a sky gone dull and turned to the house for wine

or coffee and pie. Plates clatter, and cabinets bang, and the spigot
gurgles in the sink. I'm alone on the last step, watching universal
blue darken the mountains and the sea. Over all, the voices carry

laughter through the windows open to the cool. As I sit here,
I'm laughing as they laugh, and the night unveils the keen eyes
piercing the sky deepening beyond my gaze. I'm content at the end

of a day of joy. A new bottle is uncorked, and from within, they call
my name. The stars are far, the moon far from full, yet even alone
under these old stars, I'm not alone. Now is the moment to return

to warm, yellow rooms crowded with companions, to leave the owl
hovering silent over the fallow field and the ten thousand tongues
of the starlit trees to the voiceless and eventual work the dark does.

Even Further West

There is no jay in the shrinking alphabet of birds on Maui.
No madrone, but there is kiawe and ten thousand shades

of green creeping from red volcanic soil. The mountain is

not holy, but I worship all I see. Holy is a bamboo cage
in the human head, where the mind flutters. A mountain
shaped by fire and wind and rain and the mortal machines

of men is only what you can't think it is. Sacred is best
left unsaid. Every place is sacred, but thinking so never

makes it so. The mind. All a joke. Holiness. A smug pun.
Here, try this. Show me the Buddha, and I will make him
disappear. Try again. Once more, gone. Hands are easy

to empty. The mind, not so much. Here's a red feather

from a cardinal, a cowrie from the south shore. Hold them
till your hand cramps. Hold them till your mind changes.

"The Fires Outside"
from *kindling*
(1988)

"Tonight the fires are all outside ..."
— Lew Welch

Recognition

Apparently,
I look like someone
everyone knows.

People hail and wave
across the street. I wave
back. I'm not proud.

Some approach me
speaking in tongues
I cannot speak.

I apologize
that their words are not mine,
and they apologize too.

"I'm sorry I thought
you were _____"
(the same as I am).

I am usually
pleased with being recognized
as someone familiar.

Anyone looking closely enough
will see
the resemblance.

Grandmother's Frame

There was a painting in it

            rather terrible

so we threw it away

         and hung the frame

anyway

the cracks in the wall stopped

            inside grandmother's frame

more from the attention the wall got

       than any repair of ours

and the space changed —

          the wall, the frame

and the rest of the room

           around the outside too —

so the whole house seemed different

       because of a frame we hung

but couldn't agree

      was empty

        or not.

Clearing the Library Shelves

the weight of words wobbles
the library —
        the staff strikes
titles from the catalogue
carts fat tomes on skinny wheels
       through narrow passages.

the head librarian clips
an explanation from the air —

       "I'm told," he says
       "The library is
       fundamentally, structurally
       unsound."

Buddha Fixes My Car

one response to a question concerning the method of repair

"Under the hood,
            I disconnect the battery,
        open the radiator,
                remove the air cleaner,
    and stick my fingers anywhere I can get to
                    in the motor.

I lean over and crawl under,
            look at all the belts
                and the wheels
        to make sure they're all right.

I wipe oil off the fan
                and the coil and the starter,
    and then I just look at it.
            You know, just stand and look at it.

When I start it, I go
                put my hand on the engine,
    and when it runs right, man,
            I could just kiss the carburetor."

North Beach Recognition: Today

a bear shuffling on two hind feet
walks as slow as that old woman
we passed on Taylor Street
                    not seeing her
            then both looking again —

ragged black coat with windy gray hair
her eyes and mouth
                        three circles of rapture
            actually *beholding* us.

"Look," I said,
but you were already, and I said,
                    "Good morning,"
            as we passed.

half a block later
you squeezed my hand in both of yours,
            saying, "I wonder what she saw."

        Turning
I saw her standing still
                looking after us.
                        I waved.

— a bear stands just that way scenting
                for her cubs
in meadows above the timberline
            when the first snow starts falling —

We walked on down to the water
           hoping she didn't think
we were making fun or laughing at her

as she stood seeing in us
         holding hands
  walking the sidewalk in the sun
something we really are
when we're
not thinking.

Goat Rock Beach, North California Coast

for my mother, 1927–1986

The sun rose from rock this morning
and we built a fire for company
      on the sand in spite of the light.

The waves curl green all day
        over bubbles rushing back.

We watch the sea where the sky sinks
          the ocean rises
     and falls in the rhythm of silence —

the shore alone breaks the wave.

Only here can you hear
        the voice of the surf speaking
     in tongues of sand and stones
till the sun dives seeking tomorrow.

We watch the surf until the sea is lost
        in the night
beyond our little ring of fire on the beach
     and then listen to the waves
       we can only hear.

Living at the Monastery, Working in the Kitchen
(2001)

Instructions: Do your work. Stop. Listen. Eat.
Wash your bowl. Sit still. Breathe.

●

The night Big Shield found me freezing
in the white maw of a blizzard,
my legs were numb,
my fingers frozen, bent into hooks
for coaxing blood through my body.

He laughed loudly,
and I woke
to his legs, dark columns to the clouds.

Bending low to clasp my claw,
he hoisted me
onto his back, high above the drifts.

"Come, little one," he laughed again,
"you still have work to do."

●

●

Sparrows scatter at my step
but gather round to teach
when I sit still.

They leap through leaves and pebbles,
seeking morsels, but the seed a sparrow finds
is luck
and bitter persistence, and still he looks.

The sparrow expects nothing
and finds enough.

How can I crave more?

The sparrow sees
we deserve nothing at all,
but look
at all we find.

●

●

Words wind from my mouth
     as hair winds from my head —
thick, shiny, tough lines of black
     that dirty with the dust of days,
     knot, tangle, and fall.

The bald monks grimace
when they find my poems on walls,
     on leaves, in mud, on rock,
as though seeing a single strand of black
in an evening bowl of rice.

●

•

All seem to know me here.
The Porch of Heaven rings with a name
Big Shield gave me years ago.

Pick Up's the name I'm known by,
and it's just as well. If there's another,
it's long gone now.

In the foolish abbot's face, I shout,
"But how do you know me?"

He stands on his shadow and sputters,
"I see your face every day. I know
your name. I recognize you."

Even Cold Peak thinks he knows me
at a glance.

Clearly, I am lost.

Whether I see this face
in pail or pool,
I don't know who I see.

How could I look like that man?
I don't even resemble myself.

•

•

The Way is open and free,
wide as a rice patty in Spring,
silver and broad as the face of brown water,
and unguarded as a pearl

in an oyster's open mouth, shimmering
in sunlight, among starfish and green weeds.
Yet we dare not reach
for what is free, for fear

of the unknown, the expected,
imagined menace lying
at the lip of freedom.
Instead, we cower and retreat

like an army fleeing the gaping gates
of an undefended city, only because
Kung Ming in robe and slippers
glowers from atop the wall.

•

*Kung Ming was a brilliant strategist of warfare. Legend has it that he turned aside an invading
army for which he was unprepared by throwing open the city gates and sitting in plain view
atop the walls. He was recognized by the approaching forces, who feared a trap and fled.*

●

The blazing din of summer
splits the ragged cliff.

Bright banners hang limp
in the sun.

The dull bronze curve
of the temple bell
is silent but cool to the cheek.

In the hall, monks dream
of immortality
with the shrill song

of ten thousand cicadas
ringing in their ears.

●

●

Cold Peak and I found the old man
dangling skinny legs wrapped in rags
         over a sheer granite drop
    to shadows and green below.

Laughing at the edge, waving arms through blue,
        he spurned our help, our words.
Hungry, he refused even rice we offered,
     cried he would step into the heavens
       if we came too near.

His eldest son had led him to the cliff
         but had no heart
    to shove him over ... and left him there,
but the old man's gladness shone
     as sun glows on stone.

    "All for nothing," he giggled,
    "All for nothing."

●

One ancient practice, in China and many other parts of the world, was to lead elderly people into the wilderness and abandon them. This practice was considered a humane way to deal with the difficulties posed by the old and infirm.

●

At an age now when my back
is stiff and bowed as an old broomshaft,
I dream of the dirt hut
where I was born.

My dreams are drab —
picking at the scabs
from scratching at the bites of the matbugs —
and I wake from short nights
scratching at new scabs
on thin old legs.

I will leave a pot of rice steaming
and die even as I have lived —
where I am, here —
living at the monastery,
working in the kitchen.

●

●

Young monks gaped in awe
when the old master came to meals but never ate.

Their fear was funny.
They whispered of hungry ghosts, magic kettles,
and lost desires of the holy.
I teased them with tales of one-eyed demons rising in the dark.

One night, I caught the old master
at the trap in the drain where rice gathers
when monks wash their bowls
after the evening meal.

No more rice than would fill a hermit's thimble,
yet the old monk carried
his portion to a spot warmed by the stove
and ate his meal with simple grace.

Such is the way.
Numbskulls never tire of stuffing empty heads
with grain too good for them,
while the wise survive on scraps
left by a sullen cleansing of bowls and sticks.

One wishes
the mouths of fools
might open only to shove in rice.

●

●

Books! Monks and books!

All day long reading aloud,
                    droning dead words smarter
                                        than they are.

What do they mean with all this noise?

The day the old Master stacked the library on the grass
                            and set the pages burning
        he used a single flame.

Mine was the only hand clapping.

●

●

The moon, a pearl —
what crap!

Nightly, monks stand in the yard and stare
beyond the world
at what glows dumbly in darkness.

The origin of light
reflected from that changing empty face

is ten thousand times as bright, burns colors
through earth and sky, lights the way
so clearly only a fool can lose the path.

A wise man sees the sun
is too bright to watch
and works by light whose source he never seeks.

●

●

Who works to be free
will never be free.

Raise two hands to your eyes.
Show yourself your bonds.
You see nothing.

Pity those bound by a whisper of wishes.

You are free
only when you forget
you are free.

If you seek freedom,
desire binds you,
and you are not free.

You are free.

●

●

Fire Boy talks to himself,
    all morning, trimming wicks for lamps.

"If we could run fast enough,
    we might always live in daylight
    and never need lamps.

What a bright day that would be!"

Sounds too much like too much work —
    for this ragged janitor, at least!

And if one could run that fast,
    he'd better stay in one place
    and learn the pace of day.

●

Original face. One hand clapping. Bow-wow!
    The riddle is not known for its answer.

The Savage River thunders from the peaks.
The river is not named for grassy banks on the plains.

The Way glistens on the crests of the coiling sea.
The Way is not sought for the peace we find.

And it is best not to speak of Buddhas
to one who daily watches monks eat.

●

●

After we woke,
on the day lightning struck
the pine in whose shade we sat,
my ears rang for hours
with the long, loud laughter of Cold Peak.

●

In a world of green rushes,
yellow springs, red dust, blue sky,
one need taste a peach only once
to know the savor.

●

In China, the "yellow springs" was a common euphemism for death; "red dust" was a familiar reference to the delusions of the senses. The peach was a symbol of immortality.

●

By Maple Bridge, beyond the temple walls,
a blind man mistook me
for one of these shabby brown beggars.

I stole his cane and beat him with it,
chanting sutras with the blows.

Stomping through thick red mud,
as I left, I spat in his eye
for good measure.

Who calls me a monk
can go to hell.

●

Among pines and boulders,
the path is clearest
when there is no place to go,

for through clouds and cliffs,
one goes nowhere
when there is no place to go,

and one can go nowhere
till he knows the path, too,
is a place.

●

●

Carrying ash from kitchen coals to the great heap out back,
I watched young monks gather after evening rice
in a clearing by the outhouse,
They pointed with childish, fearful cries
at a comet arcing over the Dragon's back.

One in a voice loud with the night said,
"Ancients say 'broom stars' sweep away
the old to make way for the new."
By starlight, I saw the blunt luster of bald heads
bobbing in the dark.

Like fat carp they were, thick backs breaking
a shallow surface, rushing over mossy stones to feed on scraps.

In a voice they hadn't heard
since the old master died last spring,
I crept behind them and barked, "Ho!"
The idiots bolted like frightened horses fleeing
a snaky coil of hemp curled in mud.

Fools! If a comet swept clear the walk
for every holy one born, for every throne lost, for every river
raised by rain, the sky would never be dark,
the heavens would sing with a rasp of brooms,
and dust would fly like summer stars.

●

In China, a comet, with its feathery trailing tail, is known as a "broom star." The broom, a familiar attribute of Shih-te, is also a symbol of immortality.

●

By the red pine on the verge
of the garden,
magpie, big noisy bird of black and white,
sheen of rainbow on walking wings,

squawks at windy limbs, falling cones,
glowing boulders,
and the bald skulls of brown monks
sweeping stones.

●

●

Cold Peak lectures summer grasses
                    on The Way
and disputes The Power with a bear
                    who shares his sheer sunny cliff.

His crazy laughter is a sutra
                    for the wind.

Often, I see him beaming
                    at the full moon as though gazing
on a pearl, a perfect mirror
                    of his enlightenment.

With broom, pails of water,
                    buckets of rice, and a hot stove,
I gaze at the garden I cultivate
                    for vegetables we share.

If Cold Peak had a job,
                    he might be more humble.

●

●

My pail of raw rice
is the cluttered mind of a monk.

With an idle finger, I draw
figures and characters,
       and the lines remain
till I clear the surface
          with an open hand.

After the meal,
every cooked grain
         sticks to a hand
sweeping through the rice pot,
tracing the inner curve
       of emptiness.

I am a grain of rice
stuck to the tip of a finger
      pointing to the moon.

●

New Poems

Ceremony, In the American Twilight

In college, I lived in a house with too many roommates.
      We were the bane of the neighbors with our loud,
late nights of rock, our unmown yard of grass long gone

      to seedy stalks, our primered cars of blown mufflers
and blue exhaust. One afternoon, one of us half-baked
rebels tacked an American flag the size of a loose-leaf sheet

      to the wall above a ragged couch, cinderblock
bookshelves, and cable-spool tables. From another life,
I knew when to raise and lower the colors, how to hang,

      fold, and drape the flag, all the regulations
governing the cloth we live and die for. That night,
after the rest passed out or crawled to bed, I couldn't sleep.

      I snuck into the living room and reversed the colors,
placing the blue properly on the left. Through the long days
      of the semester, the flag hung, pinned and rippling

in the occasional breeze from the front door, open, forgotten.
      The holidays came. The roommates dispersed.
Some were gone for good, and more were coming. The flag

      was in tatters, and whoever left last tore
the colors from the wall. I found the flag in the kitchen trash
      and fished the cloth from egg shells and orange peels.

      As light faded, I found an empty coffee can,
and three short, broken laths, a wad of newspaper, a book
of matches. Outside, the sun was gone. Clouds blackened

the horizon, and the blue was tempered with twilight.
In the backyard, I constructed my pyre, dropped a match
　　　　into the can, and watched flames wave at the sky.

In one hand, I held the tired flag, and I gazed into the fire.
　　　　"What you doin'?" said a small voice from beyond
the chain-link fence. The old woman next door was barely

visible, crooked in a rocker on her back porch. Caught,
I blew all my breath into the rising shadows, and said,
　　　　"Burning the flag," adding apologetically, "It's old."

A vague shape in the gloom, she paused long, then spoke
a single word, "Glory." She surprised a laugh from me,
　　　　but I had no more words. The fire in the coffee can

was snapping and glad. In the dusk, I squatted over oily earth
　　　　and gray cinders, the glitter of shattered beer bottles,
and fed the cloth into the flames. The light within showed

broad bars of red and white brilliant again when the fire
　　　　caught. Night was coming. From the faded blue field,
orange sparks rose into the darkening sky and became stars.

What's Wrong with Your Face,
Evolutionarily Speaking

a love poem

First, your face, fine, funny, or effed-up, is just another splotch
on a blank wall in the unbuilt Halls of Evolution. Look around

       the big blue and green ball that spawned us. These losers
are winners of the human race? These are the fittest? Just say no.
I'm a big fan of Darwin, but I'm ready to vote this stupid species

off the planet. Every time I finally open the yogurt again and see
that fuzzy, dusty ring of black and green on the curdy white curve,

I think hard about our ancestors, those ill-informed, bug- and grub-
eating, pit-scratching knuckle-draggers emerging from the half-lit
foulness of our origins. But you know, even naked and all, at least

they are noble enough to ignore a lack of clothes, spiffy haircuts,
make-up, piercings, and body art. The countenance of each hairy

little link gazes heroically at the horizon while we stop in every hall
       and downtown storefront to glance into each mirrored pane
of plate-glass to inspect our façades through painted letters. Look

at that lop-sided nose, those perfectly spaced, mismatched eyes,
that weirdly wide mouth of gapped and tilting teeth. God must be

an evil, little micro-manager to dis-grace each of us with that one
strange stroke we can hate about ourselves. The results often look
       so unintended we wish to call them accidents, but we can't.

You can blame no one for yourself any more than you can blame
a dropped fire hose for gushing enthusiastically and dangerously

in all directions under the pressure of a further splashy demonstration
of the urge to come forth. You can wonder why you're so beautiful
or I'm so ugly, but in the short and long run, life, in the grittiest sense,

goes on, as do landslides or tsunami, avalanches or extinction events,
and we all know disasters bring us together, so shut up, and kiss me.

On a Morning Long After Cache Creek

for Andy Ehrmann, 1960–2015

"The usual song is a 3-fold or double whistle; a simple call note
is typical. A more varied song is heard at dawn."
— *Birds of North America*

Andy took me to Cache Creek, and we hiked through afternoon
on a dim trail under oaks and pines. That day, he pointed
to my first and only Western Bluebird.
As the story goes, bluebirds are rare enough to be ironic,

and seeing one is luck, but Andy saw three that day. I finally saw
a bluebird on the way back. The water was low, and at sunset,
we strode across the creek bed in our boots. In the middle,
I stooped to pick up a rounded rock with a stark and striking

sedimentary pattern, and I watched my wet fingerprints fade
from the stone. I was there only once, and I realize now
there are places I am never going back, no matter how many days
the light brings. The blues songs all begin, "I woke up

this morning," and dawn bears the bad news. Beneath a red sky,
the bliss of night disappears into the darkness of our open eyes,
and the stars shine on without us, beyond the blue curtain
day draws between us and the truth. But night always returns.

As we were leaving, I heard the three notes and looked up.
Andy pointed, and the bird perched right where anyone lucky
might see. The back was blue, with a collar of rust, and shoulders
hunched beneath the coming night. I have not seen another since.

Lettered Among the Stars in Heaven

A is the answer, where all begins, as unclear as any alpha offered
by our ancestors. B is nothing to be desired, pollinated, seconded,
leaves all to be stood and understood or not, as a bumpkin stands
in a muddy pen of pigs, befuddled by slim glimpses of the eternal.
C is the velocity of light, squared or cubed or worse, leaving stars,

falling in every direction away from us, in the awkward position
of proposing Heaven without providing one. D is deep and distant,
like seas and stars, like mouths and questions and glasses, and time
is her companion. E is energy, of course, the first letter of my first
name, and the grade inexplicably missing from the typical list. F is

the initial of the word we love to hate and hate to love, bringing us
together to come together. G is the squeak a country bumpkin bleats
in astonishment and embarrassment to avoid addressing God. H is
the horse in the bumpkin's lofty darkened barn and heroin and house
and hankering and halo, all that we ride or rides us. I is the infinitely

capitalized integer we speak when we each speak of one of ourselves,
looking for something to say. J is the I that limps, a nifty fabricator,
a prospector of lines and lineaments, most familiar and recognized
least among us. K is potassium, for no earthly reason for those of us
who know one language alone, a pearl and a king among lesser letters.

L is for "Look," the first word I learned to read, as in "Look, Jane, look.
Look, Dick. Look at Spot." I will. I will. I will. M is the first break
in the airy stream of vowels, recognition in lips pressed thin and longing,
ma, ma, ma, oh, sweet maiden, now matron. N is the one that replicates,
in power, in thrones and dominions infesting celestial spheres no one

but rulers believe in. O is the one round mouth of the universe, empty
of nothing and what we believe, full of what we fear and love, open-
ended as a perfect, purposeless destination. P is the pint among the p's
and q's, when we sneak away to relieve ourselves. Q is an inventor
of gadgets as well as the tedious questions in a long line of interviewers

and inquisitors and the letter voted least likely to succeed. R is for *rain*
and *reign* and *rein,* which together embody a neat and sweet existential
Gordian lover's knot in a strip simultaneously single- and double-sided.
S is more, in addition, on the other hand, opposes singularity except
in action with the other, proceeds with precision in alternating curves

and current. T is a cool drink with mint and ice, sunlight gold in a glass.
U is the other, the one I addresses, silently commands, imperiously
ignores, relentlessly seeks. V is the twin of U, making a point as sharp
as a bumpkin's whistle calling cows home. W is the crone, the ancient
who's forgotten her own name, thinking she's two of one she's not,

losing all she's got and begot. X is the signature of the unknown, marks
the spot, frames the crucified, the transfixed, the now and the then. Y is
yes, yes, yes, yes, yes, yes, vital answer to every event. Z is Zed,
the country bumpkin who squats in a shed, chaw in cheek, line in creek,
blank of eye beneath a sky from which he fears G looks down on his life.

How to Love Your Enemies

homage to a fierce Ukrainian woman

Walk slowly along the forty miles of tanks
      jamming narrow country lanes
between farms of wheat, barley, and corn

open to the horizon. Spend daylight pacing
the dirt of the land you love and urging
      the invaders to return home to lovers,

sisters, and mothers who long to welcome
      a retreat with embraces and kisses.
As you go, offer a handful of sunflower
seeds to each armed man. When the soldiers

die, the flesh, blood, and bone will become
      new soil as these boys are buried
with pockets full of seeds for the future
      green fields radiant with sunflowers.

My Lame Superpower

I glow. That's all I do. All the time, night and noon, I emit constant rays
that scientists agree are equal to a thousand watts. In daylight, I shine
with a golden nimbus, a halo that makes me gleam like a Renaissance god

on a ceiling. In moonlight, I bring the blush of the sun. Moths worship
my every step, circling me as I blaze beneath stars. When I sleep, I am

my own night-light. When I can't, I'm a lamp to read by. Among all
my fellow heroes, I am the least. For the mighty, striding the comic-book

pages of the world, I'm a figure of fun, the one with no costume, brilliant
and naked in my illumination. These brave defenders of truth control wind
and weather, fire and ice. They surf the airless void and breathe underwater.

They retrieve revolvers with magnetic hands. They have respectable names,
like Wolverine, Storm, or Mr. Fantastic, and I am flippantly known as Glow.

They say, "Flame on!" or "It's clobbering time!" What can I say? "Keep on
glowing"? "Let there continue to be light"? Yet these heroes allow me
a seat at the council table, though I am little use for the colossal battles

between good and evil they plan for themselves. I sit beside the Invisible
Girl, whose power is even more ironic than mine. She's already a woman,

she once joked, who needs to be invisible? We stifle our laughter within
the lofty halls. We whisper during meetings, snort and giggle helplessly
at nemeses and evil plots we have no power to confront, oppose, or defeat.

While the stalwart champions of justice strategize, we invent silly names
for ourselves: Glass Gal, Glimmer, Pane, Sparky. Yet she keeps me honest

about myself. If superpowers can be simple, she says, mine is. Where I am, darkness has no dominion. I lead the lost through the night surrounding us.

Where I look, there is nothing I can't see. Shadows flee when I approach. My light is neither charge nor reflection. I shine from within, inexplicably and inexorably radiant. I illuminate the way for all. If you seek, follow me.

The Atheist, Shopping for Groceries
on a Friday Night
(In a Heaven in Which None of Us Believes)

In the express check-out line at Foodland (eight items or less),
Hitch rolled his cart up behind us. Since no one survives death,
        we were surprised to see him. He looked good,
in gray jacket, open collar, black slacks, and his hair grown out,
lank and gold, falling across his forehead as we remembered.

We nodded since he knew we knew him, and we thanked him
        for his hard work and good words, which have often raised
our spirits. He smiled at that. The minutes dragged, the line
locked behind a woman with three squalling children and a check.
I pointed to the "8" above him, noting that the number looked
like infinity standing on its head.

                He found that mildly amusing
in the manner Americans find so charming in British intellectuals,
responding that at least the figure wasn't lying around on the job
        as is typical of such a character. The line stalled again
behind a teenager clutching an energy drink while slowly counting

change into the cashier's palm. Veronica unloaded our spinach,
beer, and yogurt, and the three of us grinned often and awkwardly
at each other. He was gracious but seemed anxious to pick up
        his cigarettes and pay. My wife noticed a bag of kitty litter
in his cart and asked after his cat. Hitch said the cat was an orange
tabby, a male, and Veronica asked for the name. "Smith," he said.

We were all pleased. We gathered our bags to go, and he wished us
a good day, though evening darkened the doors. Among the bottles
of wine, loaf of bread, and wheels of cheese on the rolling black
conveyor were six silver cans of cat food, the special of the week,

and we walked into the darkness, smiling, glad to know
that when he arrived home, someone was at the door to greet him.

First Grade Art

In the first grade, I failed: I couldn't draw. I worked
my narrow palette of crayons to fashion curved lines
in the shape of a cat or a rocket or a dragon or a tree,

but none came to me that didn't disappoint my visions.
I was confined to a two-dimensional paper universe
where the best I could do was create a crooked family

of rectangles and ellipses beside a white box with a red
triangle roof and blank quartered cubes for windows,
a waxy house whose dimensions were always too small.

The bottom of the page was a smear of green, and the sky,
the whole sky, took all my blue and darkened everything
but the swollen yellow and orange sun I had never seen

so big and brilliant but in my own childish illustrations.
Even the stick figure I saw as myself was drawn too large
to turn the moonish knob on the slant-framed brown door

and enter the darkness within, unseen and uncolored.
A green ball on a brown stick was a tree that didn't
stand in our front yard, and on that steep-sloped roof

was a chimney aswirl with the enthusiastic black smoke
I knew from fairy tales always promised fire within.
I trimmed my little life with a box of eight cramped colors.

The miracle was my insistence on stars, not only the one
we see all day, but the two thousand that score the sky
after the one we roll around rolls away. Doggedly, I drew

yellow pentacles and asterisks through my corrugated
blue day, filling the sky with the light beyond the light.

Roger That

one for R. K.

Yesterday, I heard one of my students died. I remember
talking to him after class under stars in the parking lot
as he sat on his Harley.

           The announcement arrived weeks
late in a burst of static, and I stared through the window
at mountains draped with night to make sense of the news.

The man was my student fifteen years ago and three years
younger than I am. In class, he was scrappy. At first,
         he refused to believe words can mean enough

to hurt, but I convinced him, inventing the word "motor-
bicycle" to describe his ride. He laughed hard and said,

"Please don't say that again." I loved him for shared humor
and skepticism, and when he chose the classroom, I counted
        his students among the lucky ones. The physicists say

somewhere in the universe, a sun explodes every second,
       and the one blasting into big light in his last instant
must have been huge. I'm growing older every second, too.

I love the ticking, but what I can tell you about the sweeping
red hand is this: even death gets old. Time passes, and I meant
to send words sooner, but not everybody has a bike, man.

The Man Who Lost His Middle Finger

The man who lost his middle finger didn't think much
                                        about the empty space
            between his wedding ring and the finger

he used to point out his wife's flaws. He saved little
            time in clipping only nine nails, and he wasted
                        even more dealing with that one ass

at every party who finally drank enough to ask.
                        His loss did not make him compassionate

            toward others who lost cats or kids or countries
as their lives stripped them daily of their dignity

            and their delusions. His patience wore thinnest
in the ordinary, faded fabric of typical encounters
                        with other drivers on the highways

and boulevards he sped, and when they were stupid,
                        as he so often thought they were,
            he just used the other hand.

The Laureate and the Cockroach

We listened from the edge of light beaming down
on his gray locks and lowered lenses, and into the circle
bright on the stage crawled an enormous cockroach.

The day was chilly. The insect labored and paused,
heavily and often, antennae waving like batons in the fists

of a deranged conductor directing the grave tempo
of a poet's notes. Together, we crossed three hundred lines
and a long hour of creeping from the dark and braving

the cold. Laboring over the boards, the cockroach had nearly
reached the far edge of shadow when the words were done.
From the poet's gracious nod, we knew he did not know

the difficult journey we had made before him and his work
that day. Stepping from the podium, books and papers

in hand, fumbling glasses, he stood before us on the stage.
Looking down, he quickly crushed the insect with his shoe,
and with a brief smile, he bowed, accepting our applause.

The Hole in Your Head
Where My Voice Should Be

Jesus died, and I didn't even notice. I guess because we never spent
that much money or time together. Both of us were from the *wrong*
wrong side of the tracks, the two nearly mutually exclusive, the poor

and the stupid sides of town, bordering and even sharing a few graffitied,
weeded, smashed-glass blocks in common, but still pretty much different
neighborhoods in a grid locked with too much human traffic to recognize

anyone, in a jam or otherwise. So I'm thinking I want people to notice
when I'm gone, when I'm dead, sliced, diced, stitched, and incinerated,
even though I will be in every breath you take. After all, who notices air?

Ick, I taste the tailpipe carbon and the bulldozed refuse and the heady
scents from the waste treatment facility lighting on the tongue and filling
the cavities in my human skull with unwelcome information. I don't want

you not noticing my non-existent knocks, phone calls, e-mails, and letters.
I want there to be a troubling lack, a gap in the chawing jaw of your life
that you tongue again and again between bites, thinking about the hard,

shiny, tough grinder that used to be there. I want you coming home
to a stack of dishes in the sink and knowing I would have done them.
I want you walking to the mailbox retrieving mail from which greetings

from me will be missing and remembering I would have leaned that stack
against the sugar bowl on the kitchen table for you. I want you looking
at the night sky, trying to remember which lights I told you were planets

and which were stars, then gazing at the galaxy approaching at 250,000 miles an hour to meet ours well after the sun swallows Earth. I want you wondering what I would have said or screamed or joked or written

about the collapse of this bridge or that government or this movie star or that wall or this market. I want you to know what everything means without me, but to know you don't know what I think everything means

now. I want to see an Eric-sized hole in your life where I used to stand. And in your ears, I want black dots centered in targets of spiral cartilage on both sides of your head, at which I once aimed pointed words irritating

and illuminating. I want your ears to gape with amazement as the silence rings musically and monotonously with pointless noise that is notably, endlessly, and regretfully empty of my voice. How am I doing so far?

Portable Planet
(2000)

DIRECTIONS: As a literary supplement, peruse three pages daily. Remove inner seal. Twist off. Squeeze. Heat to boil. Stir vigorously. To preserve quality and freshness, crack volume regularly. Expose to light. Open here.

CAUTION: CONTENTS UNDER PRESSURE.

This volume is designed for all poetry readers and makes ten thousand and one suggested-strength 3-page servings. Your satisfaction with this poetry is guaranteed, and questions or comments about these poems are welcome. When writing, include ISBN on back of volume. Send correspondence to eshaffer@hotmail.com.

Best when purchased immediately. Not for resale.

Welcome to the Planet

a greeting to newborn humans

This day, we welcome you.
We teach our ways to greet you.

We are one kind among many the world encircles.
Touch all gently.

Our people are near us always.
Find yourself among the best.

Cities display our inventions and designs.
Watch, wonder, and wander away.

Highways are dark and long, concrete and crowded.
Make your own way.

Birds and beasts bring news of the planet.
Good news for your ears only.

The sea foretells the past and future.
Live now.

Soil is the source of the great and the humble.
See the small creatures close.

Mountains reveal nothing lasts.
Make peace with this.

Rivers flow in the direction of days.
Mark the many courses well.

Woods are where the world breathes.
Breathe deeply.

We greet you as your way begins.

Welcome to the planet.
Welcome home.

Indian Petroglyph State Park, Albuquerque, New Mexico

"Probably Not Christian Influence, As
The Cross Is a Universal Design Motif"
— *sign on trail*

About the time my ancestors were hauling marble around
        for some cathedral in Europe
  or making paintbrushes for Michelangelo,
      somebody who knew this place
          squatted before this black volcanic rock
  chipping this design onto this face.

Meaning maybe a star shone brightly overhead here
      or marking a significant event at this intersection
of the ten directions — a solstice, a vision, a falling star,
                an uncommon bird.

     A patient hand made these images without a plan —
thoughtfully unaware that Christians crossing the sea
      would build a fence around this *malpais*
          and make this ground a park.

     Today, I saw my first Loggerhead Shrike —
black mask, thick dark beak, silver head, black wings
      with a shock of white in the unfurling —
          perched on a wire fence
    next to a lizard impaled on a barb,
       just like the book says.

On the Often Unremarked
Advantages of Baldness

What grows up must go bald.
Yet from this hairless height,
> gleaming vistas of the future appear
when you boldly glow where no skin has shown before.

See what I mean? The glory of the sun
> sets the shedding head ablaze.
The horizons of one's sense of humor
> broaden as swiftly as hairlines recede,
for the bald head is the bare butt
> of every joke.

Look around.
Everyone sees the naked truth sparkling on the scalp.
> There's no point in splitting hairs,
and the bald facts have their benefits:

One may amass
> without criticism
> a spectacular collection of goofy hats.

No one ever forgets the color of your eyes.

The bald man knows rain falls
> with the shock of the first drop.

One may chant with brats in the schoolyard:

"No more shampoo, no more comb,
　　　　no more hair upon my dome.
No more haircuts, no more styles,
　　　　no more nasty barber smiles."

A gleam from the bean grants license to revise
the accidental anthems of youth — apologies to CSNY.

　　　　Sing along:

"Almost bought some hair,
　　　　it happened just the other day.
Gettin' kinda bald, 's gonna buy myself a toupée.
　　　　But I didn't, and I wonder why.
I feel like letting my sun-spot shine.
I feel I should show it to someone."

Scholars even teach
Wisdom herself reigns within the tonsure
　　　　Age clips around the crown.
And spiritually, the time-shorn shine head and shoulders
　　　　above the rest. The empty pate
is the glossy sign of the pure at heart.

Bald, you may be humbled by the true dimensions
　　　　　　　　of the skull,
but a certain resemblance to the cosmic egg
　　　　leads many to believe men of radiant cranium
more enlightened than they really are.

The sheer error in such assumptions is plain enough,
　　　　　　　　but with little thought,
the skullful may turn this to advantage
　　　　by keeping the head bowed
　　　　　　　and the mouth shut.

Silly youth may hallow
                  the hollow halo on your head,
may salute the colors of aged skin brave against the sky
                       for a few amusing years,
before Death creeps in with rusty scissors
to clip the naked skull so close
             a headstone fits like a marble hat,
and from your hairless head, at last, grows grass.

Instructions for Your First Poem

This is your first poem. You can use it for many things.

It may keep you dry in a sudden storm.
You can take notes on it.
Make a list. Fold it and let it fly.

You can see through it. It's a window to this world.

You can learn to read with it. It may teach you
colors and numbers and shapes.
You can review the sounds of farm animals with it.

Do not use it wisely or sparingly. Don't be careful with it.
Bend, fold, and articulate.

You can use a poem over and over and over
again.
It will always be the same.

Mark it in pencil like a familiar doorjamb.
Every year, when you stand next to it,
you'll see how much you've grown.

How I Read Poetry

When I finish reading
the book

I crumple
    the sales slip
      I used
to mark my place

and throw it away.

Death Mask in Red for Allen Ginsberg:
April 5, 1997

Poetry is a stop sign —

either you get it or you don't.

Surprisingly few do.

After all, how many drivers

ever really come

to a complete stop?

Reckless as Botchan

Coming to Okinawa, I am reckless
as Botchan leaping from the second floor
proving he could fly without dying
or slicing a thumb to try the bite of the blade.

What do I know of Japan?
Nothing but my address in Shuri, the number of my bus,
how to apologize, count my change, excuse myself, greet my neighbors,
and who is on the thousand-yen bill.

The people who live here warn me, "You will never be Japanese."
Fine, but I know where I am.
I only want to be native anyway —
to drink *Orion* or *awamori* and watch the moon,
gaze into the green and deep dragon waters of *Ryu-tan*,
know the birds, the trees, the rivers, the back roads, and the beaches.

No matter how hard I scrub my feet in the public bath
there is American dirt worn into the heel.
I won't wear shoes here either.

I know I'll never walk down the street in my own neighborhood
without taxis tooting
or finding myself the point at the end of a child's finger —
a curious man from a curious land.

"That's the way it is," I say to the children
standing at the bus stop
staring at the sky in my eyes,
"you are what you are."

But when I go back to America, I want my face
on the five-dollar bill
just like Soseki on the *sen'en-satsu.*

Hari Natal di Indonesia: *Kuta, Bali*

On *Jalan Legian,* muddy street of schemes
  and baseball-capped vendors
    of cheap watches and perfume,
      the sky is sacred blue.

The sidewalk gleams in grime. Every dirty puddle
    shines. Every filthy inch of asphalt,
every fold in the tattered skirts of black and white
        wrapped at the waists
    of stone guardians at timeless shrines
glows in the boom of noon.

From the sidewalk, shops are dark,
          stark with shadow,
    but when we linger, voices call —

      "Hello."
            "Yes, have a look?"
    "Where are you going?"

Veronica unfolds sarongs of earthy tropical hues,
          rich, dark shades in sunlight,
    and jokes with a shopkeeper
              in Indonesian.

"Ini suami saya," she says. I know the words,
          and I glance up.

He greets me, and appropriate to the day,
    I speak my little Indonesian,
          "Selamat Hari Natal."

"Oh, *Meri Kerismas,*" he says,

        "and you are Christian?"

Surprised, I blink and look at the sky. This blue

        spans a land of ten million gods,
    yet every foreign face must follow only one.

Blue and yellow taxis honk in the streets.

        Motor scooters and buses blast by.
I shake my head, searching for words

        in his language or mine,
    but find none before he asks again.

    "Buddha?"

I consider the endlessly amusing possibilities.

        Me, a Buddha?
    But I must say no. *"Bukan."*

The shopkeeper frowns, confused,

        but soon brightens.

    "Yes, Hindu."

O, land of boundless possibility! I swear

        I will instantly convert!
    But I deny him again,
      "Maaf, Bapak, bukan."

Veronica explores racks and rows of clothes,

        smiling at our slow words
    and finally speaks,
    "Bapak, dia tidak punya agamah."
    "Sir, he has no religion."

I'm astonished, amazed. No religion!

        Veronica laughs at my fallen face.

"At least tell the man I'm a poet," I whisper.

She grins, "I don't remember the word."

Now, the shopkeeper smiles.

He has an answer at last.

"O, begitu," he says, *"Dia bebas."*

"He's free."

A Portable Planet

from Shuri to Sarasota

Most of the time, we live on different days.
Our seasons match,
but your night is my day.

As I rise, you set a clock to wake you while I watch the sun set.
The only star you see when I sleep is the sun.
On New Year's Eve, we spend fourteen hours in different years.

For my birthday, you shipped an Inflatable Globe.
I unfolded seas and continents and wondered at a flat Earth.

A god who wanted everyone to see the same sun
would smash the planet to such a plane —
a single side, all edges, corners, and straight rivers.
Cartographers and generals would love it.

But the world I want is a ball,
tangled in the paradise of paradoxes
roundness generates.

So I blew it up and began to play.
The uses for a portable planet are endless.

With my fingers placed on our two towns,
I spin the globe on new poles,
a wacky axis for the plastic Earth to wobble on,
whirled without end.

Sometimes, I bounce the planet on my fist
with a rubber band looped through the North Pole.

And, yesterday, I arranged a rainbow
of plastic dinosaurs at the end of the hall
                          and bowled them over.

The world works really well this way,
         with a little english on it.

On the Verge of the Usual Mistake

I learned the same thing on the beach again.
Between the sea and the land is a broad white span
                    where the surf makes lines
                              and the lines are blank.

On the sand, hermit crabs, broken coral, and wave-worn shells,
            a cowrie with colors fresh from deeper water.

This is the margin change demands of the world.

In the surf, there is a distance before the coral grows,
            before the fish begin, where there is no rock or green.

The empty sand above and below the waves is the space
the tides mark for the moon. On the sea's blue edge
nothing grows, nothing rests,
                              nothing that comes here,
stays here.

Yadokari: *Hermit Crab, Okinawa*

He borrows his house, as I borrow mine.
$\qquad$ We are strangers where we live.

This little crab makes me think
I would crawl around the world with my belongings on my back,
$\qquad$ drag my life behind me every day,
$\qquad\qquad$ to live
in the same world of open sand, empty shells, brilliant blue.

In hand, the hermit crab lives up to the name,
$\qquad$ a shell closed with claws
$\qquad$ but a warm breeze of breath will bring him out.

Set on the shore, he works a way through humps of white sand,
broken branches of coral, sun-bleached beer cans,
$\qquad\qquad$ human footprints.

Life is kind. Move on. Carry what you can.

A Million-Dollar Bill
(2016)

"Keep the change."

Watermelon Seeds

Setting the first icy slice on my paper plate, my mother warned me
not to swallow watermelon seeds. A vine would sprout from my navel.

For the rest of my life, all would ask only about the fruit sprung
from beneath my shirt, waiting for my curved, slender sentences as long
        as the flourishing vine. All I know is this. A tough cord

of broad leaves burst from my belly. Flowers folded into fruit
and swelled with wet, pink flesh, sugar, and light, every one a world

        within a smooth, striped rind in a green as deep as summer.
Each slick, black seed between sticky fingers was as ripe with promise
      as a period, all those flat, black dots, an ever-lengthening ellipsis

leading to a day I might speak of the mystery erupting from my guts.
        All summer, I swallowed every seed.

Matching Coffee Mugs

for Veronica

At first light, a francolin calls in the field. The cat watches us wake,
speaking the moment our eyes open. Windows pale, and we rise
to start our morning chores. We work together. You feed the cat.

I make the coffee. I set our matching mugs on the kitchen counter,
your name on one, mine on the other. We shower. You carry

spiders in cupped hands to the door and release them in the roses.
I follow you and check the papaya tree. One is ripe. In the dawn,
the skin is golden. You stand by me, and we gaze at the mountain

where the sky glows. The sun soon will reach the ridge. Inside,
I bring bowls and spoons to the table. You tie the curtains back.

A cardinal lights in the kiawe tree. Our eyes open to each other.
I slice fruit on the board, and you toast the bread. I pour coffee
from a brimming pot. You drink from my cup. I drink from yours.

The Glad Reaper

In fields great and green as new grain, Death grins
as he swings his scythe, and why shouldn't he be happy?

He has the best job in the world. He's got benefits.
He's productive and appreciated. He frees the suffering.

He awards the meek their inheritance, and he drives
the proud to ground. His fences are true, long and strong,

and there's always enough rain. He's the local agent
for Evolution County. He knows all about crop rotation

and curving his furrows to fit the slope of the soil.
Darwin is his guide, God's on his side, and he cannot lose.

The sun shines on his daily labors. The wide sky
is relentlessly cheerful blue. The few clouds are chubby

seraphs that give the infinite a glad character
and bring occasional shade to his work. Death wears

the classic overalls, always new blue nearly black,
loose and stiff, with plenty of pockets, buttons, and loops

for tools. He has a hobby: he collects last words,
though few are worth hearing. The last words of most

are a fervent curse or a bleat of surprise, but Death
has a fine sense of humor. He gleefully seeks the ironic.

With a smile, he recalls Goethe croaking, "More light!
More light!" Death is immortally happy. He will outlive us

all. He sweeps a scythe that will never ever sever
his own slender neck. He's nearsighted. He carries with him

spectacles he rarely wears, and he never sees
a face till he's a heartbeat away. This evening, comfortable

in the farmhouse parlor he still calls a drawing room,

he'll don those glasses. He'll pour himself a whiskey neat,
> settle in a doilied armchair, pleasantly over-stuffed,
and chuckle in a cozy circle of lamplight over poems taunting
> his pride and his strength, his fierce and lazy grace.

The Famous Poet's Wife

At the podium, the famous poet is having sex with his wife
in the poem he reads tonight. He uses the four-letter word.

The act is all ankles and elbows, slits and staffs, grunting,
sweating, and unnaturally assumed positions. Naturally,
I'm embarrassed because I can see the famous poet's wife

squirming in her chair as he caresses the heft of her breast,
the eager spread of her knees, and a tiny, beautiful blemish

none of us will ever see. Handy with his tongue, he speaks
of that moment her thighs muffled his ears in her passion

and lingers on a lonely moment when her rush of pleasure
left him behind. The ladies are glassy-eyed. The men nod
and grin. I'm shifting in my seat. The famous poet's wife

slumps as the last line kisses the poet's lips. Some of us clap,
and the applause raises her husband's head from his work.

The Lessons of Midnight

Since we must celebrate death, let us
                 leave it to the children.

We'll cradle bowls of coins and candy,
            awaiting a knock at the door,

while they learn the lessons of moonlight
        from fallen leaves and caramel apples —

    to enter a darkening world
            dressed as monsters,

    to read fate in sidewalk cracks
        through holes in plastic masks,

    to seek treats with pretty threats
        at the doors of strangers.

The Word-Swallower

There is no charge for admission to the green, mildewed tent
staked slackly in an alley of the midway between a cotton candy
cart and ping-pong toss. Billed an attraction, the word-swallower

is not. Few come to observe him, seated on a steel, folding chair,
beneath a single spot in a vacant, shadowed, curtained room,
enshrined in silence. He swallows words. His silence is golden.

No matter how keen the verbiage rising to his tongue, no matter
  how many edges on each unspoken word that comes to mind,

his tent is hushed but for the whispers of visitors who mark well
his silent line of lips. He answers no questions, retorts to no quip,
responds to no riposte, and his attendant dog-faced boy at the door

tells every dusty bumpkin a grim, dismal tale. Says the boy,
  "If there were a king of the carnival, a lord of the boardwalk,

the word-swallower is not he. He hasn't spoken since he learned
  to talk. With no words for his wisdom, he speaks none.
Philosophers divide our sullen species from the other chimpanzees

  by the power of speech, but the word-swallower knows finer
and says naught on this or any other subject." The word-swallower

denies nothing. He fears no loss in lack of speech. He keeps peace
battened like a castle under siege and guards an armory of lustrous
weapons best left beyond reach. From imaginary battlements, each

word slips behind the tongue, lies sunk in the gullet, plummets
  to the gut. Lips sealed, tongue unbitten, his thought hardens

beneath the red fist beating the bars of his chest and the bellows
burning breath into a world soundless and pointless without words.
At dusk, the word-swallower and dog-faced boy stroll

into the hills of a trim town noisy with streetlit night. The boy barks.
The word-swallower strokes the curly fur on the boy's ears,
creeping through charged darkness and the grandiloquence of stars.

Monopoly

Monopoly is a game for winners, not for artless players like me.
I rolled the dice without thought or plan, aiming for exotic places

like Oriental Avenue, which I would fail to purchase. I spent
money and turns and favors to do something elegant like own all
of the red avenues of Kentucky, Indiana, and Illinois, ignoring

the opportunities where I landed. Or I would buy both utilities,
the Electric Company and the Waterworks, instead of keeping

one eye on the market and the other on my cash. Or I bargained
for all four railroads, especially the Short Line, with that wondrous,
intriguing name, instead of purchasing more rewarding property.

Not once did I win. Years later, my brother revealed he'd stolen
hundreds of thousands from the bank. That didn't surprise me
since he was, in those days, a kid. What startled me was the barely

repressed pride, even glee, at his success in thievery and his joy
in the undetected crimes. On that board, I spent an age as short

as a lifetime, circling the same square block on the same streets
with a racing car, a Scottish terrier, and a thimble for companions.
I slowly paid the rising rents to those who had purchased first,

income tax on that square I never missed, even the luxury tax,
always right before I got paid. Later, I watched stunned as cute,
little, green neighborhoods were replaced by ranks of red hotels,

and prices shot up even more, and my cash dwindled to thin bills
of yellow, pink, and white. In the end, I found myself penniless

and amazed, with only one shoe and no direction, in the middle
of some street of strangers, like Pacific Avenue or Marvin Gardens
or Park Place, one roll too far from another payday, sunk and glum

beyond the smirk of prosperity, lost, mystified, and three bills
from broke, counting the last of my cash into my brother's hand.

A Festival of Crescents

one for Andy

On the day of the eclipse, he was well on his way when the sky darkened.
The first shadow was like a cloud across the sun, but the darkness grew.
He would never reach home in time to cast the dwindling image on a sheet

of paper, not with pin and glass still on the kitchen table. Darkness swelled.
The birds grew quiet. A chill breeze carried the wail of a distant siren, eerie

in noon twilight. Newscasters warned never to stare at the sun. Even a peek

at the shadow devouring light might blind, but he wanted to see darkness
make a moon of the sun. He walked beneath an oak, staring at the sidewalk,

and there, a festival of crescents flickered at his feet. Thousands of glittering
images of the sun refracted through living leaves, and his was a path through
the shifting shape of light as darkness plunges through the heart and emerges.

River Eye

When I stood on the deck above the rivers I loved, felt the wheel turn
in my hands, and stared down at the shifting, murky, muddy curtain
where the Sacramento and the American became one, I was happy

to be where I was. I spent days alone on the deck of the *Damnation*
or drove the *California Kid* against the current into sunset, watching
red-shouldered hawks in cottonwoods overhead. If I did anything

right in those days, it was finding the right things to love and loving
them till they were gone. The world is no better or worse for me
passing through, or for passing through me, bent like the rays sunk

in deep water and glimmers of golden motes in the clouds of silt, soil,
and mud stirred by the flow moving the earth. Everything escapes me
now, so I drop a line into the river, catch what I can, drag snapping,

quicksilver muscle on deck, and stare for a moment into the cold,
tilting, silver-rimmed darkness of an alien eye from the river bottom
before I release at last what I never meant to catch and cannot keep.

How I Lost My Library Card

This kid at the library was reading aloud to himself in the corner,
and some old man reading the sports page — wasting time on men
who play with balls for money! — told the kid to shut up, a library,
he said, was supposed to be *quiet,* so *be* quiet, for God's sake,
and of course, in his mind, there was no doubt about who God was.

When I saw the poor kid's surprise, his embarrassment, his shame,
I finally spoke. I said, "Man, *you* shut up. Look, you grumpy fool,
what we have here is a kid reading. He's *reading!* These days,
that's a goddamn miracle. Thirteen hungry, homeless people live
on the library lawn, and you're upset because he's reading *aloud?*

Listen, you dumb bastard, silent reading is for the dead! Are you
hearing me? His lips are moving because those words are alive.
He's speaking aloud because what those words need to revive them
is his breath. He's using his voice because all that story needs
to be heard *is* his voice. So I have an idea. Toss the newspaper

in the trash, and go *play* some damn basketball, instead of sitting
on your flabby ass gazing at numbers about games you never saw.
And while you're at it, find this poor kid a chair, get him a platform,
a podium, a pulpit, put him on a pedestal to shout from his book
in the strongest voice he can raise, and ask him, no, *beg* him, to read

to you, to me, to the library staff, to the patrons, to the thirteen ravaged souls on the street, and to the rest of this vast, distracted nation. Let him read his book to us all and make us all one people for once concerned about what really matters. Let his voice lead us through a story we need to hear! Let him read! Just let him *read!*"

Man Overboard

after a painting by Christian Krohg

At the hatch, the boy grips bulkhead steel and terror
      in both hands, howling out the terrible news
with the anguish disaster forces from our mouths.
      He is alone on deck, on his first watch,
in the moment of misfortune. But I am not he.

Nor am I the man at the table, so startled in taking
his tea that he pours as the ship rolls, forgetting
      to set the cup beneath the scalding stream,
yet to notice the splashing on the board before him.

      Nor am I the cook, neck arched, head tilted
to peer from the small service window to the galley,
tears already springing to his eyes. And I'm not
the new man interrupted asking after his breakfast,
mind as blank as a student's slate, wiped clean by crisis.

      I am not the cook's mate, shirking dirtier work,
shifting listlessly through a box of oysters for one
easy to pry open, dreaming of a pearl, hearing words
that shock but do not grieve him, already plotting
      to sneak to a quiet berth below and steal a nap.

      Nor am I the bearded man
at breakfast with his newly risen mates, now nodding

after the night's duty, weary and grateful for the bells
that ended his long, dark watch at dawn.

And I am not the captain, glass in hand,
conning the crew, appointing duties to busy the hands
with work through a dim, dull day of sailing
for the far fishing grounds to set and haul the nets.

And though I wish I were, I am not the one at ease,
content with pipe packed and gripped in his teeth,
breathing in the scents of cherry tobacco,
planning a rescue, even as he sets the match to strike.

No, I am the ninth man, the one fallen in the waves,
he whom the boy has deserted to run for the crew.
I am the man he has forgotten to cast the white ring
hung behind him on the bulkhead
as I choke and spit on the face of crashing fathoms.

I am he gripped by the freezing green sea,
ice already crusting my hair, cold piercing my flesh,
drinking the heat from my heart and hands beating
at the deep as if this were a fate I might oppose alone.

I am the one unseen, adrift in the fading wake,
kicking boots away and wiping salt from my eyes
to raise them to a slick, black hull
and a deck empty of providence. I am lost,

beneath a gray sky in a sea of light and shadow
with a dark vessel sliding silently past, poised
for the moment the draft or the depths drag me down,
the maws below feast on my limbs, or the line is cast,

and I am drawn from breaking seas, dripping,
to stand on the deck once more, wrapped in wool
and sipping brandy, among my hapless companions.

A Million-Dollar Bill

on hearing of the incident in North Carolina

Nobody at Wal-Mart knows anything about the really high
denominations of bills. After all, those red-jacketed losers
work for minimum wage, and they probably never even saw
a hundred-dollar bill. I have. They're real pretty, especially
those new big-head Franklins. A million is a magic kid-dream,

like "I wish I had a million dollars." There must be a bill for that
beautiful number, so I made one for me. The one thing I can do
is draw, so I got some green ink-pens, measured a piece of paper
with a dollar, and went to work. I copied numbers and signatures
from the one I had and added all the warnings, seals, and capital

Latin quotes. I traced lines and designs, every word: "This Note
is Legal Tender for All Debts, Public and Private." That sounds
official. I even used Bill Gates in the portrait. Who else, right?
The face and backside took me a month of Saturdays to finish,
but when you're making something valuable, you take your time.

Plus, you know, the wife and kids were driving me crazy, five kids
dragging me to soccer games and malls and drive-thru windows
all the time. And I always need to keep a little peace with the wife
or at least hold life down to a dull roar. Now, folks will be joking
about that. One reporter said a million is like me and my family,

one trailed by a bunch of zeroes. Funny. At the store, I needed
to spend enough to make the bill convincing, so I loaded the cart
with a microwave oven, thirty or forty rolls of toilet paper, some
toothpaste, dog food, a gross of Pampers, and some new DVDs,
Ocean's Eleven, The Great Train Robbery, and *The Italian Job.*

The wife's been wailing for years for a new vacuum cleaner,
so I picked one of those up, too. When I got to the check-out,
I handed over that beautiful bill, green with patience and promise,
and while the cashier held my work up to the light, I stood there
in line, grinning, thinking about all the change coming my way.

RattleSnake Rider
(1990)

"Language is speech. Any other form, the printed one or the taped one, is a translation of language. All poems are translations ....

"That is language. Speech. The din of the tribe doing its business. You can't control it, you can't correct it, you can only listen to it and use it as it is."

— Lew Welch

"All the poets studied the rules of verse,
and those ladies rolled their eyes."

— Lou Reed

Instant Mythology

"Instant Mythology"®

           said the package —
you laughed and pointed to the warning

     "Not to be Taken Internally"

       and read the instructions in your own way:
"Just drop capsules in warm-slash-hot water
           and watch mythic figures arise!"

   "Fun — Educational — Non-Toxic"

      Revelations in lukewarm water!
Characters cut from colored sponge
                burst the runny plastic
     touch the water, fill, and grow large.

      You did one, I did one.

We invented magic words
         and whatever we said worked.

  Not that you got the one you hoped for —
          that night,
   I made the creature you wanted appear.

    You gave me the one with wings.

An Irregular Ode to the Idea of My Pierced Ear

dedicated to Horace and Pindar

I. The Apostrophe: First, One Side

Oh, Ear! Hear me!
Calling all ears, *listen!*
Hear me speak of the piercing of the masculine lobe!

Early on, the reactions were mixed —

"Did you get your hair cut?"

"Did you get new glasses?"

"Do you expect to get a job
with that thing in your ear?"

And there was the guy who said
after a moment of silence,
"You must be getting serious
about your poetry."

One does not make a hole in oneself lightly.

In spite of being Reckless,
piercing my ear took a decade of debate.
Then one day, I announced to my friends,

"I'll pierce my ear when I find
the right ear-ring."

So my friend holds one up and says, "Is this it?"
And I had to admit it was the right one.

II. The Catastrophe: Then, My Side

I pierced my ear with the prick

             of conscience

I pierced my ear for the music of the spheres

I pierced my ear to make a point

             of my tongue

        for piercing other ears

I pierced my ear so I could tell you to stick it

I pierced my ear for the recognition

I pierced my ear to know how it feels

           to be a man among men

I pierced my ear because the tattoo parlor was closed

I pierced my ear with a blue ball-point pen

I pierced my ear for John Wayne

I pierced my ear because my best quality

           is my tongue

I pierced my ear because I had to do something

I pierced my ear so I could see

           in the dark

I pierced my ear because I want to hear

         the whole round of sound

      slide down the gutter

    into the hole in the side of my head

I pierced my ear to live up to the name

          of Reckless

I pierced my ear because Todd found the right ear-ring

          for the left ear

I pierced my ear because I love connection

I pierced my ear so the river wind would whistle through

I pierced my ear to make way

         for the EAR-rational

I pierced my ear to confuse the opposition

I pierced my ear because women love me

> for it

I pierced my ear so I could check

> the Native American box
>
> on the application form

I pierced my ear for Vincent Van Gogh
I pierced my ear because it was stuffed

> with a wad of words on paper

> nobody ever said

I pierced my ear to make a whole in my soul
I pierced my ear to pay the price of freedom
I pierced my ear as proof I can hear

> what you're saying

I pierced my ear because my friends said

> it was a bad idea

I pierced my ear to know my rights

> from what's left

I pierced my ear because it was there
I pierced my ear to make your ear *ring*

III. The Antipode: The Dark Side of the Head

O, there is so much *concern* about piercing the right ear —
No, not the right ear!
The right ear is the left ear.

So They say.

O, Ear, listen and learn the little poem
for straight males who decorate their heads:

"Left is right; right is wrong
Left is right; right is wrong."

Otherwise, right *is* right.

But since I appeared bespiked to the world, people say,
"What the hell did you do that for?"

I always answer, "For the rest of my life."

Eric Shakespeare, Poet

for William Shakespeare,
a relative of mine

O, William, sweet William,
Should I change my name to Shakespeare?
I'd precede you alphabetically in the card catalog.

Our names are pretty close already, I guess,
and the legalities of changing names
                    might kill
                              the desire for direct descent —
          even from such a glorious Renaissance grand-sire.

But then again, Will,
who could ignore a contemporary poet
          with the thundering name of Shakespeare?

"Eric Shakespeare, Poet."

The name has a nice ring to it, don't you think?

There are so few repeaters among the famous names of poets.
          Think about that, Willy.
                    (Sure, Jonson and Johnson — big deal!)
          I'd be a *sensation!*

People would buy my books accidentally
                    and read them in confusion.

I'd be interviewed on *Donohue*

      as one of "The Most Eligible Bachelors in America."

I would sit right next to Rambo —

         the killer, not the poet.

Just think, Bill, fellow poets would jest about my right to the title

      remarking wittily in beautiful letters

           about coincidence

      and sneer behind my back at parties.

My government would ignore me until my hair was gone

         or gone white

      then summon me to Washington, D.C.

to name Shakespeare, the Poet Laureate of the United States.

They would have me write, mine William, an occasional poem

      for the inauguration of some future anonymous president.

I would read the poem on live national TV

         dressed in a black winter coat

      with rain beading on my bald head in January

and the Heads of State nodding behind my bent back.

I will scandalize the nation by forgetting the new president's name.

      I'll do it on purpose.

As a Grand Old Man of Letters, Billito, my death will be attended

      by unknown poets of the next century

         who will come because they know they should

and will write me elegies like Auden's for Yeats.

There will be a brief flurry of embarrassment

      while the officials seek a Poets' Corner

        to dump my body in.

And, Billy, when I'm safely dead,

the scholars will find a "dark lady" for me —

      faster than I ever found one myself.

Some will claim my works
                    were actually composed by Albert Einstein
          because of cleverly-concealed anagrams
              in the General Theory of Relativity.

Some will make comparisons of Eric and William
                  and find the former lacking —
    after all, who recalls *Cymbeline?*
                 Who reads any of the sonnets
        except 18, 29, 73, and 116 anymore?

Some reckless young critic will invent an egregious epithet for me
        remembering, Willbert, that Ezra Pound called you
             "the deer-snatcher of Stratford."

I won't even mention the ones I can think of here.
                      One might stick.

Some reverent young critic will write too respectfully
             I was a man of my times
                like no other, no doubt
writing honestly and hopefully of what I knew, etc., etc., etc.

"Only the coincidence," he will write,
               "of sharing the grand name of Shakespeare
      with our greatest English writer has kept this poet
                  from his rightful place
      among the best of his contemporaries."

If he writes this while I live, Billius,
             and sends the words to me for approval,
I will pencil in the margin,
      "This may be true, but I was always short
                   on beer money."

I will leave this bit of doggerel for an epitaph —
           a ridiculous inscription to chip into marble
       for some wayward American mutt to mark
           his place with a yellow stain:

      "Some preachers inform me all flesh is grass,
      But mess with my bones, and I'll kick your ass."

Ah, Billykins, you and I both know
           the scholars will say I didn't write it anyway.

For Veronica, Instead of a Rose

For centuries, poets have been getting it wrong.

They bring "one perfect rose" to show their love
       to their lovers, but now I think
          they were mistaken.

I saw a rose today growing
       behind the fence of someone's yard.
          The bloom was yellow edged with red,
     with the obligatory dew glistening on the petals,
       the bud pouting open high in the green bush,
so I bent the branch down to me.

There I was on the sidewalk, the flower fresh in my hand,
       but forgive me.

I couldn't bring myself to snap the stem of the rose
       so you could watch petals drop for days
          in the slow dying
     displayed in a jar on the kitchen table.

Love is nothing like a dead rose anyway.

The florist will never tape this poem to his cash register
       to sell flowers now,
     since I left the rose among green leaves.

Instead, I bring you these words,
     alive,
just like the rose.

Hawk in October: A Heresy of Recognition

The shadow touched me before I even saw the hawk

gliding ten feet above my head
then swooping up to perch on a phonepole
to look me over.

I looked for marks
to identify the species

but suddenly I thought of John James Audubon
wandering through the new world
killing animals
so he could draw pictures and name them.

White breast, brown-striped belly
head and wing-tips dipped in darkness —
I think I know
the species
but I won't name it now

after the hawk knew right away what I was
and had no name for me.

RattleSnake Rider

for Lew Welch,
for first asking the question: "What do you ride?"

i: The Wind and the Riddle

Asking myself the rider riddle for a long time without luck —

now in the rain-gray-dark dawn of a morning
beyond waiting at last
walking with the dog
through great gray rocks and astonishing green

warm rain in my face
new leaves rattling in trees

I hear words in my ear or in my head —

the wind is in your face, the breath is in your mouth

and I speak the words I hear aloud

"The wind is in your face, the breath is in your mouth.
The wind is in your face, the breath is in your mouth."

I *think*
these words must be
Earth-Maker's words   (call me what you will —
in my ear   this is the name I choose)
in my head

I wonder what these words mean till right now
I start to write

      and RattleSnake speaks

            right through my hand
   singing in my ear in my head this song —

ii: The Song of the RattleSnake

I carry poison in my mouth
>> my tongue split to the root.

I taste the air for danger
>> a jagged red flicker of lightning
>>>> bringing thunder before rain.

I go on my belly on the ground
>> where the elements meet — I prefer earth.

I live in a line and I curve to move.

I am the totem of the nadir,
>> the omega, the descent beckoning.

In descent is my safety —
>> down through the arteries of the earth,
> stone pulsing around my body,
>>> I am the breathing body of rock.

I am the tongue of fire in stone —
>> rains seeks me through cracks, splitting stone,
>>> opening the way deeper into darkness.

I bear my young live
>> so they may know first the grace
>>> of sand, sun, and solitude.

I shelter with my kind in winter
>> in rock rooms beneath the desert freeze.
> In summer, I sleep in shadows.
>> At night, I seek the warmth of rocks and roads.

I celebrate the nights the full moon makes
>> a pearl in a snakeskin
>>> cloud in a dark sky of sharp stars.

I make my mouth a world of teeth to strike,
        and I unhinge the doors of my jaws
                to swallow whole what finds me.

      Badger, Hawk, and Coyote seek my flesh
and the Sun may spear my life to the sand with a lance of light
            but these are not my enemies —
      my enemies are the hand, the heel
        the knife, the rifle, and the wheel.

I fang the heels of those who kill
           without love, respect, or gratitude.

I strike too quick for eye to follow
           after my rattle pierces the ear.

I carry the colors of the earth in the red dust
           on the diamonds of my skin.

My works are the skins I shed
        to renew myself —
          left for the hands of the fortunate
      as a sign of where I've been,
          not where I've gone.
       Hold them gently for their power.

I coil to center myself on nothing
         but the earth visible
            in the circle I make.

I live driven beyond the bounds of the human
        where the wind carries the yawp of Coyote.

I take my rattle in my teeth
        to renew the human myth of the round.

My rattle is my drum, beating time from the world
                    with the quick rhythm of the actual
                                        sound of presence.

I make a song of warning.

iii: *Warning of RattleSnake*

The dream was a simple one.

Walking down a Sierra trail with a good friend a good distance ahead, I come to a place where the path passes between a large gray boulder and a cut stump.

Coiled in the rings of the tree is a big RattleSnake, head and tail raised, watching my approach.

I think to myself, "RattleSnake will let me pass safe," and I walk boldly down the path.

RattleSnake sounds and strikes as I come between the boulder and the stump, biting my thigh and returning to coil in the sun watching me.

I think to myself, "Well, at least I can call my friend for help," and immediately I cannot speak.

I think to myself, "Well, at least I can walk on to a place where someone will help me," and immediately my legs buckle, and I sit down hard on the rock behind me.

I think to myself, "Well, at least I can sit here for a minute and think of something else to do," and immediately a darkness rises from the ground and covers me.

There is a voice in this darkness. The voice is the voice of RattleSnake saying,

When I take a rider,
I bring the power — I am the guide.

I am
not a symbol, not a totem, not a protector, not yours.

RattleSnake makes you
this present.

I give you ward; you give me words.
My voice and your voice are one voice on the same split tongue.

Think this way:

Rattlesnake is your sign and signature,
you speak and stand for RattleSnake.

iv: How Coyote Lost His Other Tail and His Only First Son

When Coyote started walking in the world he had two tails. One always was and still is stuck on his butt right over his anus so whoever walks behind him doesn't have to look at the puckered pink asterisk of his asshole. That tail tapers right to the point of Coyote's life wagging happy as a dog's tail, or stretched straight on out horizontal from his back when he's just sniffing around content with himself, or a question mark arching over his back making his balls the point when he gets mad, or when he sleeps curling all the way around his body in the safe circle the broad horizon of wild solitude provides.

Coyote had another tail connected between his eyes and curling back around his body or waving in the wind or standing up straight from the back of his head. That tail was rowdy and fought with his back tail all the time sometimes biting his body and pinching his ears and tickling his nose and covering his eyes till Coyote yipped and yawped so crazy and mad he pounded the top of his head with a rock till his eyes crossed. Little bits of stone chipped off the old rock and lodged there in his skin till that place on his head grew hard and knobby and the sound of rattling rock in there when he walked was even more trouble that tail made. He lived with that tail a long time because he loved how beautiful the tail was and how the hairs feathered out in a criss-cross brown, rust, yellow, black, and white pattern from the top of his head to the tip of that tail.

Till one day that second tail teasing him all day wrapping around his legs tripping him on the rocks made his temper so bad he wrestled on the ground trying to beat his head with stones.

"What the hell are you doing, Coyote?" says Earth-Maker. "What's all this damn ruckus in the rocks? Are you crazy or something?"

"My tail drives me crazy," Coyote yells wrestling on the ground.

"Well, why don't you just rip that tail right off?" says Earth-Maker. "Drive down stakes into the ground through the end and pull!"

Coyote found two thin slivers of rock and pounded them through the end of his tail and tried to tear out that tail by running away fast but at the end of his tail he lost his feet, snapped into the air, and slammed back on the earth because that other tail was really stuck on there. Finally he went out as far as he could and ran fast past the rock and out as fast as he could as far as he could and tore that tail right out of his head at last. If you feel Coyote's head today there's still a little ridge of bone between his ears where that second tail finally came off.

"Now I can tell one tail from the other," says Coyote dancing on the rocks and pulling that second tail out of the ground swinging it around his head whooping and beating the stones till the hair blows away in little clouds. Coyote finally whirls that tail hard around his head and lets fly into the desert.

That tail landed high in the rocks and crawled away and became RattleSnake with the two slivers of stone for teeth and the juice from the bruises of the beating for poison and the brilliant diamond designs on the skin showing now with no hair covering and the little bits of rock Coyote beat into the head of his tail for a rattle.

RattleSnake and Coyote didn't like each other at all for a long time but still RattleSnake only accidentally granted Coyote's wish to Earth-Maker one day when Coyote thought death might be a good idea to bring into the world. Coyote argued a loud and long time to bring death into the world and Earth-Maker agreed at last just to shut Coyote up. Right then, Coyote's son was running through a meadow not far away and he trod on RattleSnake. RattleSnake bit his heel in surprise. Coyote's son died from the bite and Coyote ran straight to Earth-Maker.

"I've changed my mind, Earth-Maker," says Coyote. "Death is a bad idea. Take death back out of the world."

"Coyote, I cannot take death back now. Now the world knows death and death will always be a part of the world. It's too late. Burn and learn, Coyote," says Earth-Maker.

"RattleSnake bit my son and killed him," says Coyote. "Revive him."

"I cannot revive him," Earth-Maker says. "Death is in the world now. You invented death so you are the only one who can die and revive again. You'll just have to learn to live with death, Coyote."

Coyote yips and howls crying with anger and sadness but he can think of nothing to say so he goes to the meadow to find RattleSnake.

RattleSnake sleeps coiled half in shade and half in sun on a warm rock. He hears Coyote coming through the grass and raises his head and tail watching. When Coyote stops in front of the stone, RattleSnake says, "Hello, Coyote."

Coyote says, "Hello, RattleSnake. My son is dead for all time now. Death is in the world. This is all my mistake. We have to do something right now."

RattleSnake becomes the first apologist for death.

"I'm sorry about your son, Coyote," says RattleSnake, "Neither of us saw the other till too late. Now, what can we do?"

Coyote thinks a moment about death and what to do.

"I will die many times to show people how to die right and wrong and I will revive to show people how silly it is to fear death," says Coyote looking at the raised tail of RattleSnake. "As for you, I've got a big idea."

Coyote told RattleSnake his big idea and RattleSnake agreed and Coyote's big idea still works in the world to this day. Coyote and RattleSnake are good friends now. Coyote wanders as always through the world at will still and RattleSnake always tries to sound his tail before striking now because Coyote and his children never watch where They're going when They're going.

v: *"The Wind is in Your Face, The Breath is in Your Mouth"*

> *"Fire finds its own form."*
> — *William Blake, willfully misquoted*

I dream all my works
    bursting into flame
   at the moment of my death —
so when the time comes to burn books
     burn mine first.

This request will bring my friends and my enemies together
for once.

Drag out the body of my work
and let the fire lick everything not green away.

Publish the words to the sky
and let the smoke make the sunset red.

Let the wind carry my breath in every voice
my voice in every breath.

Let the ashes make good ground.

vi: Last Will and Testament

Don't look for me when I disappear —
               you can bet my body rots in rocks
                              beyond your reach.

Finding my bones, take one —
                              make yourself an ear-ring
but keep your hand away from the skull
          grinning white in the sun on the sand —

          the rattle you hear within
                    is the sound of the actual
RattleSnake coiled in the bone globe —

                    still.

Please skip this apologia before buying the book.
Poems must speak for themselves, and I'm only the author,
so flip through and listen to the lines
on your own tongue first.
Then if you must, come back around.

Afterface,
or Light Reflected from the Back of My Head

According to Jordan, my exalted and stellar publisher, I must face one way or the other, and since I have many words and much punctuation, and I certainly don't write only for myself, I will. Had we but world enough and time, I would explain everything, but this, and only this, now.

Why Selected Poems *Instead of* Collected Poems?

I'm still alive and speaking, which means you get *Selected & New Poems.*

When I first queried my extraordinarily wise, gifted, and generous publisher about a volume of selected poems, he responded in favor and commented, "By the way, before you suggested a selected poems, I was thinking of a collected poems . . . ," so when I noted that selected was more to my taste, Jordan Jones, like a highballin' railroad engineer drivin' the Illinois Central line, cleared the tracks ahead. So call this volume, if you will, *The Incomplete Works of Eric Shakespeare.* And why, *& New?* Jordan said so.

Collected Poems are fat tomes for scholars and students; *Selected Poems* are slim volumes for readers, and I want readers, and I want to choose the best for my readers to read first. Why? In selected poems, especially this particular selection of the author, readers should expect the best work. The real draw of *Selected Poems,* whether building one or buying one, is the assurance that the poems included were actually chosen from a larger field of work with an eye toward what most engages and endures. Readers are welcome to agree, then later invest in *Collected Poems* or to disagree, then skip the *Collected Poems.*

If you like these poems, buy the seven other volumes, too, since these lines and those are exactly like mine. You're welcome, Jordan. Also, pick up my *Collected Poems,* whenever that volume is available. But don't blame me. I'll be gone. You will, however, make my publisher magnificently rich and impressively cover some shelf space in your library. You're welcome, Jordan. And if you ask, yes, Jordan may even autograph the title page for both of us. And if you don't like these selected poems, yup, you won't like the rest of my work either, so quit while you're ahead and into the void with you.

The bookstore gives me the impression that ink-stained and wretched composers of verse get, like, only one *Selected Poems* per writer, so I built this volume myself, and everything in the book is my fault.

Novus Ordo Librorum

The order of the books in this volume raises questions, and like most writers, I welcome an opportunity to think in ink. I am simply not a big fan of causation, chronology, progress, or sequence (witness *Burn & Learn,* still my favorite and only novel I ever published).

Causation, chronology, progress, and sequence imply development that is not accurate concerning literary work. Including poems in sections denoted by the books containing those works makes sense to me, but presenting the books in chronological order implies my goals and interests for my poems and writing career have advanced or improved, and that is not true.

I've never had much confidence in critical assumptions concerning the development of a poet's "voice" or "skill" or "work," especially when the assumptions and assessments rely only on chronology. When a poem was written does not necessarily relate to the quality of the work. Mathematicians may do their best work before the age of thirty, but if a writer keeps a sharp pen and a brimming inkwell, good work can appear anytime. Examining the poems written between today and the late 1960's, when I began to write, the ones I consider my best appeared randomly, in a way that I regard as achrononological.

Critics often present the unnecessary and misleading argument that the "voice" or "power" of a writer improves through the years. The power in a poem is more a function of a particular knot of now, a moment erupting above and through the quotidian. In the moment of creation generating the poem, the elements of excellence in perception, expression, and understanding intersect. Sometimes, that moment precipitates gold; sometimes, pyrite; sometimes, silver; sometimes, quicksilver. But today's poem cannot be expected to be better than yesterday's, at least not simply because this year C.E. is more recent. Implying that a writer's work progresses with age furthers the ends of criticism, not of literature. Change happens; composition happens; progress, not so much.

The minute matters less than the moment. Chronology is the arithmetical succession of seconds, but we don't create on the clock. We create in the single moment of eternity, an island of now, a lens that focuses everything we are, and in such a moment, we don't have access to eternity, we *are* access to eternity, entrance and emergence. The more brilliant the moment, the better the work. As with a lens, the light and images that pass through depend on the circumstances, aperture, exposure, focus, and scene. So some work is better than other work, not because of the age or experience of the writer, but because of the convergence of all of the elements that create a moment, of which only one is the writer, but not the most important part, and certainly not the defining part, and definitely not a feature improved by "then" in any sense.

And so this order reflects only my archipelagic intentions: starting with islands where I now live, traveling backward to islands of my past and the pasts of others, leaping forward to islands emerging in recent decades, vaulting back to the spherical island of the globe, and finally landing on my own skull, revealing that I am not an island. However, you may certainly ignore the sequence of poems here, too. Open this volume to any page, and read whatever lines you find.

Play On: Seventy-Three Words on Performing Poetry

Lew Welch called poems "scores for the voice." I agree. For us, a poem on a page is sheet music. Whenever we "play" the words, we infuse whoever we are at that moment into the notes. I rarely perform my own poems the same way twice; I add, revise spontaneously, skip, even re-arrange, words and lines and verses, making the poem new in each new moment. Feel free to do the same.

EPS
May 23, 2023
Kailua, O'ahu

Acknowledgments

Grateful acknowledgment is made to the editors of the following publications, in which these poems were first published or reprinted.

2010 Lorin Tarr Gill Writing Competition for Poetry (First Place): A Boat of Bones

The Acorn: Grandmother's Frame; Indian Petroglyph State Park, Albuquerque, New Mexico

Bakunin: On the Verge of the Usual Mistake

Bamboo Ridge: Ceremony, In the American Twilight; Illumination; My Lame Superpower; Roger That

Beloit Poetry Journal: The Famous Poet's Wife

Blue Collar Review: Of Owls and Sugar Cane

Brobdingnagian Times (Ireland): from *LATM:* "The blazing din of summer"

California Quarterly: Hawk in October: A Heresy of Recognition

California State Poetry Quarterly: Reckless As Botchan

Canary: River Eye

Celestial Musings: Poems Inspired by the Night Sky (anthology): One for the Bear; Victoria's Astronomy Lesson

Central American Literary Review (Nicaragua): First Grade Art

CerBerUs: from *LATM:* "Among pines and boulders", "Fire Boy talks to himself"; "Who works to be free"

Chaminade Literary Review: On the Verge of the Usual Mistake; Reckless As Botchan

Cider Press Review: A Festival of Crescents; Matching Coffee Mugs

COLLECT: Art/Design for the Curated: Man Overboard

Crossing Lines: A 2015 Main Street Rag Anthology: How I Lost My Library Card

Dalhousie Review (Canada): All There Is

East and West Quarterly: *Yadokari:* Hermit Crab, Okinawa

Empty Vessel: from *LATM:* "Among pines and boulders"; "Books! Monks and books!"; "My pail of raw rice"; "The night Big Shield"; "The Way is open and free"; "Who works to be free"; "Words wind"; "Young monks gaped in awe"

The End of the World Project: Welcome to the Planet; Whales at Sunset

Entering: The Davis Poetry Anthology: 2011: For Veronica, Instead of a Rose

The Ethicist: *Hari Natal di Indonesia:* Kuta, Bali; [Indian] Petroglyph State Park, Albuquerque, New Mexico

Eunoia Review: Death Mask in Read for Allen Ginsberg: April 5, 1997

Fire (England): *Hari Natal di Indonesia:* Kuta, Bali

Fire and Rain: EcoPoetry of California (anthology): River Eye

Fish Drum: from *LATM:* "All seem to know me here"

Gargoyle: Ceremony, In the American Twilight; Lettered Among the Stars in Heaven

Going Down Swinging (Australia): The Atheist, Shopping for Groceries on a Friday Night; Headlights: A Biology Lesson; A Million-Dollar Bill; Monopoly; Redemption

Green Ink Poetry: For Veronica, Instead of a Rose

Hawai'i Pacific Review: The Lessons of Moonlight

Heavy Bear: Grandmother's Frame; Lāhaina Noon; Lovers on Pūlehu Road, Between the Sugar Mill and the Maui County Dump; Mozart and the Mockingbird; Recognition; Watermelon Seeds; Welcome to the Planet

Hundred Mountain: from *LATM:* "Among pines and boulders"; "Books! Monks and books!"; "Fire Boy talks to himself"; "The night Big Shield"; "The Way is open and free"; "Who works to be free"; "Young monks gaped in awe"

Island (Australia): Arrival; Even Further West

Jack London Is Dead: Contemporary Euro-American Poetry of Hawai'i (And Some Stories) (anthology): Officer, I Saw the Whole Thing (Pushcart Prize "Special Mention" in Poetry in *The Pushcart Anthology XXXI* (2007), nomination by Antler); Whales at Sunset

Lummox: As a Shark Sees; How I Lost My Library Card; Lovers on Pūlehu Road, Between the Sugar Mill and the Maui County Dump; Of Owls and Sugar Cane

Malahat Review: from *LATM:* "Carrying ash"

Maui Time Weekly: Instructions for Your First Poem

New Millennium Writings: As a Shark Sees

Nightsun: from *LATM:* "Carrying ash" (Pushcart Prize nomination by Barbara Hurd, editor)

North American Review: The Famous Poet's Wife; How I Lost My Library Card

Oregon Literary Review: Watermelon Seeds; Witnesses

Pearl: Lāhaina Noon; North Beach Recognition: Today

Pinchpenny: Buddha Fixes My Car

Pleiades: Indian Petroglyph State Park, Albuquerque, New Mexico

Ploughshares: Mozart and the Mockingbird

Poetry NZ (New Zealand): River Eye

Poetry Pacific: All There Is

PRISM International (Canada): Lovers on Pūlehu Road, Between the Sugar Mill and the Maui County Dump

Prole (England and Wales): The Man Who Lost His Middle Finger

Prose Ax: from *LATM:* "Words wind"; Lovers on Pūlehu Road, Between the Sugar Mill and the Maui County Dump; A Portable Planet (Winner of the 2000 Potent Prose Ax Prize for Poetry; Pushcart Prize nomination by Jhoanna Calma Salazar, editor)

Pudding Magazine: The International Journal of Applied Poetry: Hawk In October: A Heresy of Recognition

Quadrant Magazine (Australia): The First Man to See A Rainbow

Quantum Leap (Scotland): *Yadokari:* Hermit Crab, Okinawa

Queen's Quarterly (Canada): What's Wrong With Your Face, Evolutionarily Speaking

RATTLE: For My Sake; Officer, I Saw the Whole Thing; The Word-Swallower

Redstart Plus: "Instant Mythology": Epiphany, 1988

The Rose Book: For Veronica, Instead of a Rose

Salt Hill Journal: The Hole in Your Head Where My Voice Should Be

Seawords: Arrival; As a Shark Sees; A Blue Curve; Goat Rock Beach: North California Coast; Lāhaina Noon; On the Verge of the Usual Mistake; Welcome to the Planet; Whales at Sunset; *Yadokari:* Hermit Crab, Okinawa

Slant: How to Love Your Enemies

Slate: Sitting in the Last of Sunset, Listening to Guests Within

Spillway: The Glad Reaper

Stick: An Irregular Ode to the Idea of My Pierced Ear

The Sun Magazine: Illumination

talking gourds: On the Verge of the Usual Mistake; Welcome to the Planet

Tar River Poetry: All There Is

Terrain: On the Verge of the Usual Mistake

Threepenny Review: from *LATM:* "Words wind"

Tor House Newsletter: Victoria's Astronomy Lesson

Tule Review: Reckless As Botchan

Universal Oneness: An Anthology of Magnum Opus Poems from Around the World (India): All There Is

Weatherings (anthology): *Yadokari:* Hermit Crab, Okinawa

Weber: The Contemporary West: Five Planets at Once; On a Morning Long After Cache Creek

ZZZ ZYNE: from *LATM:* "Young monks gaped in awe"

About the Author

Eric Paul Shaffer is author of seven books of poetry. More than 600 of his poems have been published in the USA, Australia, Canada, Costa Rica, England, Germany, India, Iran, Ireland, Japan, Netherlands, New Zealand, Nicaragua, Scotland, Singapore, and Wales. A few of his poems have been translated into Esperanto, Farsi, or Spanish.

His poems appear in twenty-seven anthologies, including *Fire and Rain: EcoPoetry of California* (Scarlet Tanager, 2018), *The EcoPoetry Anthology* (Trinity UP, 2013), *Jack London Is Dead: Contemporary Euro-American Poetry in Hawai'i* (Tinfish, 2013), *100 Poets Against the War* (Salt, 2003), and *The Soul Unearthed* (Tarcher/Putnam, 1996).

Shaffer's first novel *Burn & Learn, or Memoirs of the Cenozoic Era* was published in 2009. Other fiction appears in *Bakunin, Bamboo Ridge, Natural Bridge,* and *News from the Republic of Letters,* and in two chapbooks, *You Are Here* (2004) and *The Felony Stick* (2006).

Shaffer received Hawai'i's 2002 Elliot Cades Award for Literature to an established writer; a 2006 Ka Palapala Po'okela Book Award for *Lāhaina Noon;* the 2009 James M. Vaughan Award for Poetry; a 2010 Lorin Tarr Gill Writing Competition Award for Poetry (first place); a 2019 Ka Palapala Po'okela Book Award for *Even Further West;* and 2020 Lorin Tarr Gill Writing Competition Awards for Nonfiction (first place) and for Poetry (third place).

Shaffer received a poetry fellowship to attend the 2006 Summer Fishtrap Writers Workshop. In 2015, he was a visiting poetry faculty member at the 23rd Annual Jackson Hole Writers Conference in Wyoming, and has been a returning presenter, delivering the Keynote Address in 2013, at the Ko'olau Writers Workshops sponsored by Hawai'i Pacific University.

Shaffer lives on O'ahu and teaches composition, literature, and creative writing at Honolulu Community College.

Praise for the Poetry of Eric Paul Shaffer

Even Further West (2018)

"In *Even Further West,* Eric Paul Shaffer weaves a garland of narrative and lyric eco-poems gathered from the fallen blossoms of his experiences in Hawai'i. After journeying through this book, you will see the illuminated depths of our sacred ecology, our boat of bones, our living breath."

> — Craig Santos Perez, author of the *From Unincorporated Territory* multi-volume series, *Habitat Threshold, Navigating CHamoru Poetry,* and Winner of the 2011 PEN Center USA Literary Award for Poetry

"Shaffer is Hawai'i's Thoreau. Of the usual imaginings of Hawai'i, these poems resist the normal temptations to pare it down to palm trees and white sands. While being grounded in paradise, Shaffer simultaneously guides you to someplace deeper, someplace holier. Insightful, elegant and unpretentious, these words will make you remember the thing inside that you were born with, but lost the second you learned your name."

> — Christy Passion, author of *Still Out of Place,* & co-author of *No Choice But to Follow* & *What We Must Remember*

"In *Even Further West,* Eric Paul Shaffer beautifully locates himself and the islands of Hawai'i by means of a pleasantly apocalyptical geography of heart and mind that reaches home "in the last of the light" to unveil for us in his witty and all-seeing lyricism "the voiceless and eventual work the dark does." These are poems you will want to reread again and again."

> — Joseph Stanton, author of *A Field Guide to the Wildlife of Suburban O'ahu, Cardinal Points, Things Seen, Imaginary Museum, Prevailing Winds,* & *Moving Pictures*

"Like a cocoon, Eric Shaffer's new book of poetry transforms mundane moments and objects in nature into something transcendental, and the lines take flight from the page. In the title poem 'Even Further West,' he writes about finding a cardinal feather and a cowrie shell and says, 'Hold them till your mind changes.' Many of these poems may change your mind about the things you take for granted, maybe even the way you look at the world."

— Stuart Holmes Coleman, author of *Eddie Would Go, Fierce Heart, & Eddie Aikau: Hawaiian Hero*

"In *Even Further West,* Eric Paul Shaffer belies the self-critique that ends his poem 'Upcountry Overlook: Kula, Maui': 'I gawked at the furrowed sea and sun-scored red slopes, attentive// to the distant and dramatic, but not to significant lives / close at hand, within reach, and indifferent to our slow recognition.' While he knows well that 'the light is gone before we even know we need to see,' what he sees is instructive: we learn to appreciate the beauty of Maui, but also human pain. Among the most moving of these poems are those that allude to a broken relationship between father and son, and between the poet and himself. 'If ever there was a good time to pull a Hemingway,/ this is it,' he writes in a novena. He pulls back, declares, 'I'm not going anywhere,' and returns to writing poems attentive both to natural beauty and the compassion that comes of attending to it, as to 'the close at hand.'"

— Susan M. Schultz, author of *Aleatory Allegories, Dementia Blog, & Memory Cards* series, & editor of *Jack London Is Dead*

A Million-Dollar Bill (2016)

"Eric Paul Shaffer's poems are always filled with clear light and fresh air. They restore deep attention and gratitude, a rebalancing between land and sky."

— Naomi Shihab Nye, author of *Everything Comes Next: Collected & New Poems; Cast Away: Poems for Our Time; Voices in the Air: Poems for Listeners; Fuel; & You and Yours*

"The poems in *A Million-Dollar Bill* represent Shaffer's thoughtful presence in the world at his (and our) big-hearted best. His poems are full stories in small frames, always sharply said, never sentimental, relentlessly true, sensuously rich, always welcoming us in."

—J.D. Whitney, author of *Grandmother Says; All My Relations & Sweeping the Broom Shorter*

"*A Million-Dollar Bill* is Eric Paul Shaffer's most imaginative book yet! With unparalleled accuracy and clarity, Shaffer's astute observations turn the world on its ear through your ear. Read these poems aloud and often.

— Sara Backer, author of *Such Luck; Bicycle Lotus; Scavenger Hunt & American Fuji*

"*A Million-Dollar Bill* reached me just in time. After going without any new Shaffer poems for eleven years, I was beginning to wonder if I was going to die of thirst, reading my way across the Great American Poetry Desert. I'm okay now. Thirst quenched but hoping I don't have to wait that long again."

— Red Pine, a.k.a. Bill Porter, translator of *Dancing With the Dead: The Essential Red Pine Translations; The Collected Songs of Cold Mountain; The Zen Works of Stone House & In Such Hard Times & author of Zen Baggage: A Pilgrimage to China*

"Eric Paul Shaffer's poems must be radically *après-garde* because I swear I sometimes understand every word. It's as if Shaffer's appointed himself defender of those corniest of literary values: clarity and precision. What's more, he writes with a naive sense of wonder and play, as if poetry in our century didn't necessarily have to be ambiguous or self-canceling or dead, and earnest communication were still possible between human beings by way of mere, lovingly chosen words and images. You'd almost have to think the man enjoys being alive."

— M. Thomas Gammarino, author of *King of the Worlds; Big in Japan & Jellyfish Dreams*

Lāhaina Noon: Nā Mele O Maui (2005)

"The arrival of a new collection of Shaffer's precise, graceful, witty, luminous work makes for a happy day in the Fowler household. No one is better at peeling away a single, ordinary moment until the whole world has been revealed."

— Karen Joy Fowler, author of *The Jane Austen Book Club; Sarah Canary & Booth*

"*Lāhaina Noon* is not only a specific study of Maui, but a brilliant examination of a human's place in the cosmos. Eric Paul Shaffer's clear, sane, poems will help you understand where you are wherever you are."

— Sara Backer, author of *Such Luck; Bicycle Lotus; Scavenger Hunt & American Fuji*

"Eric Paul Shaffer's poems, well-crafted and wise, don't speak from the mind, the heart, the spirit—those are our divisions; they speak from the whole, integrated mammal he is—the sort of voice we need more of on this great Earth."

— J.D. Whitney, author of *Grandmother Says; All My Relations* & *Sweeping the Broom Shorter*

"ERIC PAUL SHAFFER, SHADOWLESS MAN OF LĀHAINA NOON—HE'S IN CAMO YOU THINK YOU SEE HIM BUT HE ISN'T THERE—HE IS LIKE EARTH SHINE ON DARK SIDE OF MOON—HE IS WRITING DOWN HIS LIFE AS IT HAPPENS—MOCKINGBIRD LISTENING TO MOZART—TRACKING BIG URSA THROUGH NIGHT SKY—HE TELLS US WHAT HE SAW WHEN SKY CRACK OPEN LIKE BLUE EASTER EGG—EPIPHANIES THAT COMPRISE OUR DAILY LIFE"

— Albert Saijo, *Outspeaks: A Rhapsody; Woodrat Flat* & *Trip Trap* (with Jack Kerouac & Lew Welch)

"Like a magic lantern, Shaffer is a bearer of light. At times his poetry becomes so incandescent it makes you just sit in wonder. The rest of the time it reveals lush landscape and uncommon wisdom. Pay attention. This is the dawning of a major talent."

— Steven Taylor Goldsberry, author of *Luzon* & *The Writer's Book of Wisdom: 101 Rules for Mastering Your Craft*

"In a career that has been building for two decades, Eric Paul Shaffer has managed to create an impressive, intriguing, varied, and highly accomplished body of published work. *Lāhaina Noon*, Shaffer's fifth collection of poetry, is a strong contender for his best book ever. Whether he is sketching the ecological metaphor of a black leopard surviving on Maui, or narrating the experience of the first human ever to see a rainbow, or dramatizing that unique celestial moment when the sun annihilates the false perspective of our shadow lives by shining straight down on our heads, Shaffer reveals to us in *Lāhaina Noon* not only the grace that allows us to inhabit and enjoy the natural world, but also the terrible responsibility we have not to destroy it."

— Robert Clark Young, author of *One of the Guys*

Living at the Monastery, Working in the Kitchen (2001)

"How wonderful to discover these lost works in the last leavings of the Twentieth Century. May their author continue to sweep the kitchens, the courtyards, the shrine halls of his always surprising mind. Thanks for the broom."

> — Red Pine, a.k.a. Bill Porter, translator of *Dancing With the Dead: The Essential Red Pine Translations; The Collected Songs of Cold Mountain; The Zen Works of Stone House* & *In Such Hard Times* & author of *Zen Baggage: A Pilgrimage to China*

"The poetic spirit connects across the centuries. Shaffer's outside/in, inside/out view is the next best thing to being there."

> — Steve Sanfield, author of *The Rain Begins Below; A New Way; Wandering; He Smiled to Himself; A Fall from Grace* & *American Zen: by a guy who tried it*

"Once again, Eric Paul Shaffer offers up to us the 'work of the moment.' In this new book of poems, he takes on monastic life in ancient China. But don't be confused or misled, these contemporary poems have enough irreverence for all of us."

> — James Taylor III, author of *Fresh Leather: The Buffalo Poems* & *Forty Years & 20 Paces*

"These poems — like a strand of black hair in the monastery rice bowl — demand our attention and irreverently remind us that 'enlightenment' has nothing to do with purity or perfection. 'Be human!' Shaffer bellows."

> — John Kain, author of *Cheater's Paradise*

Portable Planet (2000)

"*Portable Planet* is a marvelous book. I've been following Shaffer's work for years and he is on a definitive upward spiral."

> — Jim Harrison, author of *The Shape of the Journey; The Theory & Practice of Rivers; Legends of the Fall; The English Major; The Woman Lit by Fireflies* & *The Road Home*

"Graced by the best from the past, the poet wanders. His poems will take you to places you need to visit."

> — Steve Sanfield, author of *The Rain Begins Below; A New Way; Wandering; He Smiled to Himself; A Fall from Grace* & *American Zen: by a guy who tried it*

"Eric Paul Shaffer's *Portable Planet* demonstrates a nomad's sense of place around the Pacific Rim."

— Magda Cregg, author of *Hey Lew: Homage to Lew Welch*

"Eric Paul Shaffer's poems carry us ever inward and out, where particular stones sprout wings, where solid ground is shaken by the nimble fingers of small gods, and the normal everyday ways of life stay blessedly themselves. These poems are portable, they're the exact same size as the hip pocket of your mind."

— John Kain, author of *Cheater's Paradise*

RattleSnake Rider (1990)

"There is a sure, crisp sense of the line and obsession with the durable things of value on earth…. In a curious way, what I like best about Shaffer is he is not the least bit housebroken, though at the same time he is erudite…."

— Jim Harrison, author of *The Shape of the Journey; The Theory & Practice of Rivers; Legends of the Fall; The English Major; The Woman Lit by Fireflies* & *The Road Home*

"Eric Paul Shaffer is a dangerous man. It behooves you to know what he's thinking."

— Steve Sanfield, author of *The Rain Begins Below; A New Way; Wandering; He Smiled to Himself; A Fall from Grace* & *American Zen: by a guy who tried it*

"The beauty is in the bite."

— John Kain, author of *Cheater's Paradise*

kindling: Poems from Two Poets (with James Taylor III, 1988)

"If I could read, I would read *kindling*."

— Coyote

"*kindling* really says a mouthful."

— Demosthenes

"I'm following in the footsteps of the guys who wrote *kindling*."

— Sasquatch